Collins

# SNAP REVISION

## ANIMAL FARM

### AQA GCSE English Literature

PAUL BURNS

REVISE SET TEXTS IN A SNAP

Published by Collins
An imprint of HarperCollinsPublishers
1 London Bridge Street,
London, SE1 9GF

© HarperCollinsPublishers Limited 2017

9780008247133

First published 2017

10 9 8 7 6 5 4 3 2 1

British Library Cataloguing in Publication Data.

A CIP record of this book is available from the
British Library.

Printed in the UK by Martins the Printer Ltd.

Commissioning Editor: Gillian Bowman
Managing Editor: Craig Balfour
Author: Paul Burns
Copyeditor: David Christie
Proofreaders: Jill Laidlaw and Louise Robb
Project management and typesetting:
  Mark Steward
Cover designers: Kneath Associates and
  Sarah Duxbury
Production: Natalia Rebow

ACKNOWLEDGEMENTS

Quotations taken from *Animal Farm* by George
Orwell, 2000, London. *Animal Farm* copyright
1945 by Eric Blair. Reproduced by permission of
Penguin Books Ltd.

The author and publisher are grateful to the
copyright holders for permission to use quoted
materials and images.

Every effort has been made to trace copyright
holders and obtain their permission for the use of
copyright material. The author and publisher will
gladly receive information enabling them to rectify
any error or omission in subsequent editions. All
facts are correct at time of going to press.

# Contents

## Plot

| | |
|---|---|
| Chapters 1 and 2 | 4 |
| Chapters 3 and 4 | 6 |
| Chapters 5 and 6 | 8 |
| Chapters 7 and 8 | 10 |
| Chapters 9 and 10 | 12 |
| Narrative Structure | 14 |

## Setting and Context

| | |
|---|---|
| Orwell and 1945 | 16 |
| The Setting of *Animal Farm* | 18 |
| Communism and Fascism | 20 |
| Genre | 22 |
| The Russian Revolution | 24 |

## Characters

| | |
|---|---|
| Old Major | 26 |
| Napoleon | 28 |
| Snowball | 30 |
| Squealer | 32 |
| Boxer | 34 |
| Clover and Mollie | 36 |
| Benjamin, Muriel and Moses | 38 |
| Other Animals | 40 |
| The Humans | 42 |

## Themes

| | |
|---|---|
| Power and Oppression | 44 |
| Freedom and Equality | 46 |
| Corruption | 48 |
| Violence | 50 |
| Deceit and Propaganda | 52 |
| Religion and Ritual | 54 |
| Language | 56 |

## The Exam

| | |
|---|---|
| Tips and Assessment Objectives | 58 |
| Practice Questions | 60 |
| Planning a Character Question Response | 62 |
| Grade 5 Annotated Response | 64 |
| Grade 7+ Annotated Response | 66 |
| Planning a Theme Question Response | 68 |
| Grade 5 Annotated Response | 70 |
| Grade 7+ Annotated Response | 72 |

| | |
|---|---|
| Glossary | 74 |
| Answers | 76 |

# Chapters 1 and 2

**You must be able to:** understand what happens at the beginning of the novel.

## What is the setting?

The novel is set on a farm in England, which at the beginning of the novel is called Manor Farm.

## What is the situation?

One night at the beginning of March, when Mr Jones the farmer has gone to bed, the animals gather in the barn because Old Major, the boar, has had a strange dream that he wants to tell them about.

## What does Old Major tell them?

He says that before he dies he wants to share his 'wisdom' with them. He says that farm animals work hard in misery only to be slaughtered when they are of no more use. He says that the farm could support them in comfort for the whole of their natural lives. Man is their enemy. Humans do not produce anything themselves and they are responsible for the animals' misery. He tells the animals that they must overthrow the human race. Some time in the future there will be a rebellion. He also tells them that all animals are equal.

## What is Old Major's dream?

Old Major says that he dreamed of what the earth would be like without Man. During his dream, he remembered a song sung by animals long ago, called 'Beasts of England'. He sings it and the other animals join in. When the noise wakes Mr Jones, he fires his gun and the meeting breaks up.

## What happens at the start of Chapter 2?

Three days later, Old Major dies. Over the next three months, the pigs, led by Napoleon, Snowball and Squealer, prepare the other animals for revolution. They develop Old Major's ideas into a system called Animalism.

## How does the Rebellion come about?

On Midsummer's Eve, Mr Jones stays out all night drinking and when he gets back he goes to sleep. The animals have not been fed all day. One of the cows breaks into the store shed and the animals help themselves to food. Jones and his men whip the animals but the animals attack them and drive them out of the farm.

## How does Chapter 2 end?

The pigs have taught themselves to read and write. They replace the 'Manor Farm' sign with one that says 'Animal Farm' and on the wall of the barn they write the Seven Commandments. They say these will be the laws by which the animals will live forever.

The cows have not been milked, so the pigs milk them. The other animals begin the harvest. When they return, the milk has disappeared.

## Key Quotations to Learn

'Now, comrades, what is the nature of this life of ours?' (Old Major: Chapter 1)

'... before I die, I feel it my duty to pass on to you such wisdom as I have acquired.' (Old Major: Chapter 1)

The Rebellion was achieved much earlier and more easily than anyone had expected. (Chapter 2)

## Summary

- Old Major tells the animals that they should rebel.
- The pigs develop a system called Animalism.
- On Midsummer's Day, the animals rebel and drive out the humans.
- The pigs re-name the farm 'Animal Farm' and paint the Seven Commandments on the barn wall.

## Questions

QUICK TEST
1. Why do the animals go to the barn?
2. According to Old Major, what is the only animal that does not produce anything?
3. Which three pigs become leaders?
4. What do the pigs paint on the barn wall?

EXAM PRACTICE
Using at least one of the 'Key Quotations to Learn', write a paragraph explaining how Orwell describes the Rebellion in Chapter 2.

# Chapters 3 and 4

**You must be able to:** understand what happens in Chapters 3 and 4.

## What is the situation?

The animals have taken over the farm and are getting in the harvest.

## How do the animals manage the farm?

Most of the animals cooperate and work very hard, supervised by the pigs, and the harvest is very successful. They continue to do well throughout the summer, overcoming any difficulties with the help of the pigs' brains and Boxer's strength. On Sundays, they do not work but have meetings where they fly a flag and the pigs put forward resolutions, which the animals vote on. Napoleon and Snowball usually disagree.

## How do things change in Chapter 3?

The pigs teach the other animals to read and write. Not many of the animals succeed and they also have difficulty remembering the Seven Commandments, so Snowball simplifies them to 'FOUR LEGS GOOD, TWO LEGS BAD'. Snowball forms committees. Napoleon takes the new puppies from their mothers up to a loft.

## How does the chapter end?

The animals discover that the pigs are taking the milk and apples for their own use. Squealer explains that they are doing this because milk and apples are necessary for their health and that if they did not have them they might fail in their duty and Jones would return. The others accept his explanation.

## What happens at the start of Chapter 4?

The local farmers are disturbed by what has happened at Animal Farm and they put about rumours that things have turned out badly. Meanwhile, Napoleon and Snowball send out pigeons to spread news to animals on other farms. Soon animals throughout the countryside are performing acts of rebellion and singing 'Beasts of England'.

## How do the farmers react?

In October, Jones, his men and men from other farms, try to recapture the farm. Snowball organises the animals and employs defensive tactics he has learned by reading the writings of Julius Caesar. They ambush the humans by the cowshed. One sheep is killed but the animals drive out the humans.

## How does Chapter 4 end?

Snowball makes a speech by the dead sheep's grave about how animals should be prepared to die for Animal Farm. They create a military decoration, 'Animal Hero, First Class', which is awarded to Snowball and Boxer. They name the battle the Battle of the Cowshed.

## Key Quotations to Learn

... everyone worked according to his capacity. (Chapter 3)

FOUR LEGS FOOD, TWO LEGS BAD (Chapter 3)

Now if there was one thing the animals were certain of, it was that they did not want Jones back. (Chapter 4)

## Summary

- The animals successfully bring in the harvest and work well through the summer.
- The pigs teach the other animals to read and write.
- The pigs keep the apples and milk for themselves.
- In October, Jones tries to recapture the farm but is defeated in the Battle of the Cowshed.

## Questions

QUICK TEST
1. What do the animals do on Sundays?
2. Which two animals usually disagree?
3. How do the pigs let animals on other farms know about the Rebellion?
4. From which author and military leader does Snowball learn about military tactics?

EXAM PRACTICE
Using at least one of the 'Key Quotations to Learn', write a paragraph explaining how Orwell describes the way life has changed for the animals since the Rebellion.

# Chapters 5 and 6

**You must be able to:** understand what happens in Chapters 5 and 6.

## How does Chapter 5 start?

Mollie, the horse, is seen taking sugar from a man across the fence. Later, she disappears and is seen pulling a cart. She is never mentioned again.

## How do things change in Chapter 5?

Snowball makes plans to build a windmill to supply the farm with electricity. Napoleon is against the project and says that they should concentrate on food production. They also disagree about how to defend the farm, with Napoleon wanting to get firearms and Snowball arguing for stirring up rebellion on other farms. They hold a meeting about the windmill.

## What happens at the meeting?

Snowball persuades the animals to support the windmill. Before they get a chance to vote, Napoleon summons nine enormous dogs into the barn. They attack Snowball, who runs away and escapes through a hole in the fence.

Napoleon announces that there will be no more meetings. Decisions will be made by a committee of pigs. Later, Squealer tells the animals that they cannot risk animals making the wrong decision. He stresses the importance of discipline.

## How does the chapter end?

Old Major's skull is placed at the foot of the flagpole and the animals file past it every Sunday before entering the barn. Now the pigs sit on a platform, guarded by dogs, while Napoleon reads the orders for the week.

Napoleon announces that the windmill is to be built after all. Squealer tells them that it had been Napoleon's idea in the first place. He pretended to oppose it in order to get rid of Snowball, who was a bad influence.

## What happens at the start of Chapter 6?

The harvest is not as good as the previous year. The animals start to build the windmill and although the work is hard and there are some shortages, they still feel they are better off than they were.

## How do things change in Chapter 6?

Napoleon tells the animals that he has decided to trade with neighbouring farmers. The animals remember making resolutions not to deal with human beings, trade or use money but Squealer tells them this never happened.

The pigs move into the farmhouse and sleep in the beds. Clover remembers that one of the Seven Commandments forbids this, but when Muriel reads the commandment it has been changed to 'No animal shall sleep in a bed with sheets'.

# How does Chapter 6 end?

By autumn, the windmill is half built. The animals are tired and there is not much food for the winter but they are happy and proud of their achievement. In November, there is a terrible storm and the windmill collapses. Napoleon says Snowball has destroyed it. He says they will rebuild it.

 **Key Quotations to Learn**

... nine enormous dogs wearing brass-studded collars came bounding into the barn. (Chapter 5)

The dogs sitting round Napoleon let out deep menacing growls ... (Chapter 5)

The windmill was in ruins. (Chapter 6)

 **Summary**

- Snowball plans to build a windmill but Napoleon opposes it.
- Napoleon sets a pack of dogs on Snowball, who escapes from the farm.
- Decisions are to be taken by a committee of pigs. The pigs move into the house.
- Napoleon decides to build the windmill and claims it was his idea.
- Napoleon starts to deal with humans.
- The windmill is blown down in a storm. Napoleon blames Snowball and vows to rebuild it.

 **Questions**

QUICK TEST
1. What is the purpose of the windmill?
2. What must the animals file past every Sunday?
3. What are the pigs doing that Clover thinks is against the Commandments?

EXAM PRACTICE
Using at least one of the 'Key Quotations to Learn', write a paragraph explaining how Orwell conveys a sense of danger and excitement in these chapters.

# Chapters 7 and 8

**You must be able to:** understand what happens in Chapters 7 and 8.

## How does Chapter 7 start?

During the winter, life is hard on the farm and food rations are cut but Napoleon fools the solicitor, Mr Whymper, into thinking that there is plenty of grain.

## How do things change?

Napoleon makes a deal to sell eggs and crushes the hens' protest. Everything bad that happens is blamed on Snowball, who Napoleon claims was always in league with Mr Jones. Squealer gives a new version of what happened at the Battle of the Cowshed. Boxer protests but Squealer convinces him that whatever Napoleon says must be true. Napoleon plans to sell a pile of timber to one of the neighbouring farmers, Mr Frederick or Mr Pilkington.

## What is the climax of Chapter 7?

Napoleon orders the dogs to attack four young pigs. They also attack Boxer, who fights them off. The pigs 'confess' that they have been plotting with Snowball. The dogs kill them. Other animals confess to various crimes, which they say they were ordered to do by Snowball, and are executed.

## How does the chapter end?

The animals gather at the windmill, unable to understand what has happened. They sing 'The Beasts of England' but Squealer tells them they are now forbidden to sing it.

## What happens at the start of Chapter 8?

Clover remembers that one of the Commandments forbade killing animals. When Muriel reads it, it has been changed to 'No animal shall kill any other animal *without cause*'. Although the animals feel they are working harder and eating less than under Jones, Squealer gives out figures that show huge increases in production.

## How do things change?

Napoleon announces that he has made a deal to sell the timber to Pilkington. The windmill is completed. Napoleon tells the animals that he is going to sell the timber to Frederick. He says that rumours about Frederick's cruelty are untrue. Frederick's men take the timber and pay in five pound notes. The notes are forged and worthless.

## What is the climax of Chapter 8?

Frederick's men invade the farm, shoot at the animals and blow up the windmill. The animals attack them. Some animals are killed and nearly all of them wounded. However, the dogs drive the men off the farm. The pigs celebrate victory but others, including Boxer, question whether it is a victory. However, when they see the flag flying, hear Napoleon's speech and are rewarded with apples, they are convinced. It is called the Battle of the Windmill.

# How does Chapter 8 end?

The pigs find whisky and drink it. They decide to brew their own alcohol. Squealer is found at the bottom of a ladder in the barn with a pot of white paint. Later Muriel notices that the fifth commandment has been altered to 'No animal shall drink alcohol to *excess*'.

## Key Quotations to Learn

... there was a pile of corpses lying before Napoleon's feet and the air was heavy with the smell of blood ... (Chapter 7)

The banknotes were forgeries! Frederick had got the timber for nothing! (Chapter 8)

A mighty cry for vengeance went up ... (Chapter 8)

## Summary

- The pigs re-write history to make Snowball look bad and Napoleon look good.
- Napoleon's dogs kill animals who have 'confessed' to crimes.
- Napoleon sells the timber to Frederick, who pays in forged notes.
- Frederick invades the farm and blows up the windmill.
- The animals fight off Frederick's men. The fight is called the Battle of the Windmill and it is hailed as a great victory but it comes at great cost.

## Questions

QUICK TEST
1. What are the names of the two neighbouring farmers?
2. Who is blamed for everything that goes wrong?
3. How does Frederick get the timber for nothing?

EXAM PRACTICE
Using at least one of the 'Key Quotations to Learn', write a paragraph explaining how Orwell conveys fear and horror in these chapters.

# Chapters 9 and 10

**You must be able to:** understand what happens at the end of the novel.

## How does Chapter 9 start?

Boxer is getting old and should be due for retirement under the farm's rules. The rations are reduced, apart from for pigs and dogs. Squealer continues to give out positive statistics, which the animals believe.

## How do things change?

The farm has a successful year but as pigs are given more privileges, rations are again reduced for other animals. However, there are more songs, speeches and processions. While dragging a load of stone to the windmill, Boxer collapses. Squealer tells the animals that Napoleon has arranged for him to go to hospital.

## What is the climax of Chapter 9?

A van comes to take Boxer away. Benjamin reads the writing on the side of the van and tells the other animals that Boxer is being taken away to be killed. As the van drives off, Boxer tries to escape from it but is unable to.

## How does the chapter end?

Squealer explains that the rumours about Boxer being taken to the **knacker's** are untrue. Napoleon praises Boxer and the pigs hold a memorial banquet. They have found the money to buy a crate of whisky.

## What is the situation at the start of Chapter 10?

Years have passed. There are few animals left who remember the days before the Rebellion. The windmill has been completed and the farm is well organised, but the animals do not enjoy the luxuries that Snowball promised them. Only the pigs and the dogs have gained from the success of the farm. However, the animals remain proud that theirs is the only farm in the country owned and run by animals.

## What changes?

Clover is shocked to see Squealer walking on his hind legs. He is followed by all the other pigs walking on their hind legs, Napoleon with a whip in his hands. As they try to protest, the sheep start a new chant: 'Four legs good, two legs better!' The Seven Commandments have been replaced by one: 'ALL ANIMALS ARE EQUAL BUT SOME ANIMALS ARE MORE EQUAL THAN OTHERS'.

## What happens at the climax of the novel?

The pigs invite neighbouring farmers to inspect the farm. The other animals watch through the farmhouse window as the pigs and humans eat, drink and make speeches. Napoleon announces that from now on there will be no flag, no marching past Old Major's skull and that the farm will be re-named Manor Farm.

## What happens at the end?

The pigs and humans fall out over a cards game when Pilkington and Napoleon both play the same cards. When the other animals look at them they cannot tell the difference between pigs and men.

## Key Quotations to Learn

'They are taking Boxer to the knacker's!' (Benjamin: Chapter 9)

It was a pig walking on his hind legs. (Chapter 10)

The creatures outside looked from pig to man, and from man to pig, and from pig to man again; but already it was impossible to say which was which. (Chapter 10)

## Summary

- The farm prospers but most of the animals are worse off.
- Boxer is sent to the knacker's.
- The pigs start to act like humans.
- The neighbouring farmers are invited to inspect the farm and socialise with the pigs.
- The animals cannot tell the difference between pigs and humans.

## Questions

QUICK TEST
1. Which animals are better off than the others?
2. What is the sheep's new chant?
3. What three changes does Napoleon announce to the humans?

EXAM PRACTICE
Using at least one of the 'Key Quotations to Learn', write a paragraph explaining how Orwell writes about the pigs becoming like humans.

# Narrative Structure

**You must be able to:** explain the significance of the different ways Orwell has structured the novel.

## How is the novel structured?

The novel is divided into ten chapters. The story is told in **chronological** order in the third person. Orwell is an omniscient narrator, who can take us into the minds of any of his characters.

## How is the story structured?

The first chapter contains the novel's **exposition**. Through the meeting in the barn, readers are introduced to the setting, the main characters and the current situation on the farm.

When Jones fails to feed the animals in Chapter 2, they rebel. This is what is sometimes called the **inciting incident**, an event that changes everything.

There are several **turning points** or **crises** in the novel, for example, the Battle of the Cowshed, the expulsion of Snowball and the Battle of the Windmill.

The story reaches its **climax** in the final chapter when the pigs walk on their hind legs and become indistinguishable from humans.

## How is each chapter structured to keep the reader interested?

After the first chapter, most chapters begin with some exposition of the general situation at Animal Farm. For example, in Chapter 2 we are told that Old Major died in early March and his death was followed by secret activity. At the beginning of Chapter 4, Orwell tells us that by late summer news of the Rebellion was spreading around the country.

The chapters typically include some minor incidents that lead up to an important, dramatic incident. For example, Chapter 7 starts with the hens' protest against having their eggs taken away. The tension builds to a climax when Napoleon sets the dogs on Snowball. Similarly, in Chapter 9 we are told of the building of the schoolroom for young pigs and several other incidents that demonstrate how things are changing at the farm before, towards the end of the chapter, Boxer is taken to the knacker's.

Most chapters end with an incident that tells us something about how the pigs gradually betray the principles of the Rebellion and acquire more power. Chapter 2 ends with the milk disappearing; Chapter 3 with the pigs acquiring the apples; Chapter 5 with Squealer lying to the animals about Snowball; and Chapter 7 with the changing of another commandment. Often, the animals are left puzzled by these incidents and readers are left to work out what is really going on.

## Key Quotations to Learn

Old Major, the prize middle white boar, had had a strange dream on the previous night and wished to communicate it to the other animals. (Chapter 1)

And when they came back in the evening it was noticed that the milk had disappeared. (Chapter 2)

All that year the animals worked like slaves. (Chapter 6)

## Summary

- The novel is divided into ten chapters.
- There are several important turning points in the plot.
- The story reaches its climax in the final chapter.

## Questions

QUICK TEST
1. In what order does Orwell tell the story?
2. Give an example of a turning point in the story.
3. What do the incidents at the end of chapters usually tell us about?
4. What happens at the story's climax?

EXAM PRACTICE
Using one or more of the 'Key Quotations to Learn', write a paragraph analysing how Orwell uses structure to involve the reader in the story.

# Orwell and 1945

**You must be able to:** understand how the novel's meaning has been shaped by the author's reasons for writing the novel and the time at which it was written.

## Who was George Orwell?

Orwell's real name was Eric Blair. He was born in 1903 in India to a British family.

He served in the Imperial Police in Burma, lived in Paris for a while and fought on the Republican side in the **Spanish Civil War**. During the Second World War (1939–1945), he worked for the BBC and served in the Home Guard.

*Animal Farm* was written during the Second World War and was published in 1945. Orwell's other great novel, *Nineteen Eighty-Four*, in which he imagines a future Britain as part of a huge **totalitarian** state, was published in 1949.

He died in 1950.

## Why did he write *Animal Farm*?

When Orwell wrote *Animal Farm* Britain was at war with Nazi Germany. Orwell was a **socialist** and had fought against **fascism** in Spain. People were aware of the dangers posed by such right-wing regimes, both to their own people and to the rest of the world.

Many British people, particularly socialists and what Orwell called 'the intelligentsia', supported **communism**, as practised in the **USSR** (or Soviet Union). Orwell felt their support was hypocritical. Left-wing governments, such as Stalin's in the USSR, could be as cruel and dangerous as right-wing ones. Orwell had seen evidence of this from his own (losing) side in the Spanish Civil War. However, Britain and the USSR were on the same side and any criticism of the USSR was discouraged.

## What was the reaction to *Animal Farm*?

Orwell found it difficult to get the book published. Left-wing publishers did not like the fact that it was clearly an **allegory** of the Soviet Union. Others were concerned about its effect on morale while the war was still on. After it was accepted for publication, there were delays because of a shortage of paper and the book finally came out when the war was over.

## What was the world like in 1945?

After the defeat of Germany in 1945, the world changed dramatically. Eastern European countries came under the influence of the USSR, becoming communist. They remained communist until the 1990s. There were fascist governments in Spain and Portugal. Other countries, such as Germany and France, returned to democracy. In Britain, a Labour government was elected, which started a programme of **social reform** in accordance with socialist principles.

## How was *Animal Farm* received?

*Animal Farm* was a success from the moment of its publication. Some saw it simply as an allegory of the Russian Revolution and the corruption of communist **ideals**, but Orwell himself said that, although it was a **satire** on the Russian Revolution, it was intended to have a wider application.

## Summary

- Orwell wrote *Animal Farm* during the Second World War.
- Britain and the USSR were on the same side in the Second World War.
- Orwell felt that criticism of Stalin and the USSR was not allowed.
- He intended the book to be about more than just the Russian Revolution.

## Questions

QUICK TEST
1. In which war did Orwell fight?
2. According to Orwell, which country did the intelligentsia support uncritically?
3. Which party came to power in Britain in 1945?

EXAM PRACTICE
It was a source of great satisfaction to him, [Pilkington] said [...] – to feel that a long period of mistrust and misunderstanding had now come to an end. (Chapter 10)

Relating your ideas to the historical context, write a paragraph explaining how Orwell portrays the relationship between Animal Farm and the neighbouring farms.

# The Setting of *Animal Farm*

**You must be able to:** understand how the novel's setting reflects the themes of the novel.

## Where and when is *Animal Farm* set?

*Animal Farm* is set on a farm in England, near a fictional town or village called Willingdon, around about the time of writing. The action takes place over several years. Orwell always tells us what season it is and what the weather is like when something happens.

Two neighbouring farms are mentioned: Foxwood, owned by Mr Pilkington, and Pinchfield, owned by Mr Frederick.

## What is the farm like?

Animal Farm is a typical early twentieth-century farm. It is run by one man, who owns it, and a few 'farm hands'. The farm does not have electricity and there are no tractors, horses being used to pull ploughs and other farm machinery.

## What are the main locations in the farm?

The farmhouse and other buildings are arranged around the farmyard.

The farmhouse is seen by the animals as a place of 'unbelievable luxury'. They agree that it will be preserved as a museum and no animal will ever live there. However, in Chapter 6, the pigs move in. Here we see the pigs become more and more like human beings, and in the last chapter, the other animals watch through the windows, **symbolically** separated from the pigs, as they entertain the humans.

In the farmhouse garden the flag is raised, guns are fired on special days and the animals file past Old Major's skull.

The yard is the location of the Battle of the Cowshed in Chapter 4, so called because the animals hide in the cowshed ready to ambush the men. It is also where Napoleon orders the executions in Chapter 7.

The barn is where the animals assemble in Chapter 1 to be addressed by Old Major. After the Rebellion, when regular Sunday meetings are held there, it becomes symbolic of the animals' freedom and equality. Napoleon's increasing power is shown when he sits on the platform in the barn surrounded by dogs.

The Seven Commandments are painted on one of the walls of the barn. Later, a poem in praise of Napoleon is inscribed on the wall opposite the Commandments.

Other events take place in the henhouse (the hens' protest in Chapter 7), the stables (the destruction of the symbols of **oppression** in Chapter 2) and the store shed (the start of the Rebellion in Chapter 2).

The windmill is built on a small **knoll** in the long **pasture**. It becomes an important symbol, representing the animals' hard work and sense of achievement, but also a sense of frustration and the pointlessness of their work. It is intended by Snowball to supply electricity but instead is used to mill corn. However, the animals still view it with pride, gathering there for comfort after the **purges** in Chapter 7. The windmill is built from stones hauled from the quarry.

External locations include the **orchard**, where Old Major is buried and from which the pigs take the apples in Chapter 4, and a small **paddock**, which is set aside for retired animals but is planted with barley in Chapter 8.

## Key Quotations to Learn

They rolled in the dew, they cropped mouthfuls of the sweet summer grass, they kicked up clods of the black earth and snuffed its rich scent. (Chapter 2)

It was also more suited to the dignity of the Leader [...] to live in a house than a mere sty. (Chapter 6)

... they gambolled round and round the windmill, uttering cries of triumph. (Chapter 8)

## Summary

- The novel is set in a typical early twentieth-century farm in England.
- The pigs moving into the farmhouse is an important moment.
- Locations such as the barn and the windmill acquire symbolic meanings.

## Questions

QUICK TEST
1. What decision do the animals make about the farmhouse after the Rebellion?
2. Where do the executions take place?
3. Which building represents the animals' hard work?

EXAM PRACTICE
Using at least one of the 'Key Quotations to Learn', explain how Orwell uses a description of a place to create **atmosphere** and convey important themes.

# Communism and Fascism

**You must be able to:** understand how the ideas and practice of communism and fascism are reflected in the novel.

## What is communism?

Communism is the idea that property, especially the **means of production**, should be held in common by all the people. This idea has been around since ancient times. The **Industrial Revolution** of the eighteenth and nineteenth centuries caused the rise of **capitalism**, meaning most property and, therefore, power, were in the hands of a minority of people. The majority (the working class or **proletariat**) only controlled their own labour. Marx and Engels wrote about how the working class could gain control and how resources should be shared equally in *The Communist Manifesto* (1848).

These ideas were developed by Lenin (see page 24). After the Russian Revolution, the government of the USSR **nationalised** industry and agriculture, so property now belonged to the people in theory. The USSR was a one-party state, meaning there was no real democracy, and the Communist Party controlled all aspects of life.

After the Second World War, most Eastern European countries were communist. Like the USSR, they abandoned communism at the end of the twentieth century. Countries that still follow versions of communism include China, Vietnam and Cuba.

## What is socialism?

There are many different forms of **socialism**. What they have in common is a belief in social ownership. The British Labour party was founded as a socialist party. Most modern socialist parties support democracy and do not reject capitalism altogether.

## What is fascism?

The term 'fascism' is usually applied to political parties and systems that are strongly nationalist – believing in the strength of their own country – and **authoritarian**, concentrating power at the top, usually in one person (a dictator). Fascist countries are often characterised by violence.

In the mid-twentieth century, Germany (under Hitler), Italy (under Mussolini) and Spain (run by General Franco), were fascist countries. It is now very rare for people or parties to refer to themselves as fascists and it is often used as a term of abuse.

## What is totalitarianism?

Totalitarianism refers to a system of government where the state tries to control every aspect of life. Therefore, it can be applied to both communist and fascist states.

# How are these ideas reflected in *Animal Farm*?

At the start of the novel, Old Major expresses ideas similar to those of communism. The rest of the novel shows what can happen when these ideas are put into practice by a corrupt government that betrays its ideals and its supporters. Mr Frederick's farm is like a fascist state.

Orwell shows how similar communism and fascism can be in practice. The problem is not communism itself but totalitarianism. He does not show a positive model of society, except briefly just after the Rebellion.

## Summary

- Communists believe in holding property in common.
- Fascists believe in authority and nationalism.
- Both systems are characterised by state control of all aspects of life.

## Questions

QUICK TEST
1. Do communists support capitalism?
2. What system do China and Cuba follow?
3. Name three countries that used to be fascist.

EXAM PRACTICE
'Why then do we continue in this miserable condition? Because nearly the whole of the produce of our labour is stolen from us by human beings.' (Old Major: Chapter 1)

Relating your ideas to the historical context, write a paragraph explaining how Orwell portrays Old Major's political philosophy.

**You must be able to:** understand *Animal Farm* in the context of literary traditions and genres.

## What is genre?

Genre is a French word meaning 'kind' or 'type' and is used in English Literature to group texts according to style and subject matter.

## To what genre does *Animal Farm* belong?

*Animal Farm* has been described as a fairy story, a **fable**, an allegory and a satire. It contains elements of all these genres.

## How is *Animal Farm* a fairy story?

The novel was subtitled 'a fairy story' by Orwell. The term refers to a traditional story intended for children, from which they might learn moral lessons. It usually has a child-like **protagonist**, clear ideas of good and evil, magic and a happy ending. Some fairy stories, such as *The Three Little Pigs,* feature animals.

Like fairy stories, *Animal Farm* has uncomplicated characters and is set in world where extraordinary things happen, such as animals talking. Otherwise, it has little in common with fairy tales and Orwell may have meant the subtitle **ironically**. Orwell did not use this subtitle for editions published outside Britain, partly because it made some people think it was intended as a children's story.

## How is it a fable?

The story is more like one of Aesop's Fables. These stories feature animals who talk and act as humans, while keeping the characteristics of the real animals (known as **anthropomorphism**). Orwell's use of animals is similar. Fables teach clear moral lessons. Although Orwell does not tell us directly what the lesson of his story is, it can easily be **inferred**.

## How is the novel an allegory?

An allegory is a story with a second meaning partly hidden by its literal meaning. In traditional allegories, **abstract** ideas (such as Love or Justice) are **personified** as humans. Allegories were often religious, for example, *The Pilgrim's Progress* (1678). Writers in the seventeenth and eighteenth centuries also used allegories to **satirise** politics and the public figures of the day.

Orwell follows this tradition. *Animal Farm* is an allegory of the Russian Revolution and its aftermath. Many of the animals and events in the novel are clearly based on Russian leaders and the history of the USSR. However, Orwell made it clear that *Animal Farm* is not just about Russia: its lessons can be applied to other revolutions and totalitarian states.

# How is the novel a satire?

Satire is a way of writing that criticises people, institutions or societies indirectly by making fun of them. Orwell referred to *Animal Farm* as a satire. It is not primarily a comic novel but there are elements of humour, such as when the pigs walk on their hind legs and dress up. By turning the pigs into animals who do ridiculous things, Orwell satirises the Soviet leaders. He also satirises their institutions (for example, in the absurd titles given to Napoleon) and their whole society.

## Summary

- *Animal Farm* is subtitled 'a fairy story' and contains some elements of the genre.
- Fables use animals to teach moral lessons, as does *Animal Farm*.
- The novel is an allegory of the Russian Revolution and its aftermath.
- *Animal Farm* uses satire to expose the USSR and similar regimes.

## Questions

QUICK TEST
1. What is the subtitle of *Animal Farm*?
2. What are the main characters of Aesop's fables?
3. How does satire criticise people and society?

EXAM PRACTICE
Twelve voices were shouting in anger, and they were all alike. (Chapter 10)

Relating your ideas to ideas about genre and literary tradition, write a paragraph exploring how readers can infer moral or political lessons from the last chapter of *Animal Farm*.

# The Russian Revolution

**You must be able to:** understand how the events of the Russian Revolution are used in *Animal Farm*.

## What caused the Russian Revolution?

Russia was ruled for centuries by absolute monarchs, the Tsars. During the reign of the last Tsar, Nicholas II, there was a lot of discontent, caused by poverty and hunger, and a desire for greater equality. Conditions for the people got worse after Russia entered the First World War and there were many strikes and **mutinies**. The Tsar abdicated but could not prevent the Bolshevik Revolution of 1917. The Bolshevik Party, led by Vladimir Ilych Lenin, seized control of the country.

## How is this reflected in the novel?

Mr Jones is like the Tsar. The animals suffer under his neglect and have no rights. Old Major represents Lenin, who urged the workers of the world to unite against their **oppressors**. Old Major's **idealistic** vision of a farm without Man is similar to Lenin's vision of a world after revolution. The Battle of the Cowshed parallels the Russian Civil War when a variety of groups, including supporters of the Tsar, tried to overthrow the Bolsheviks.

## What happened after the revolution?

Lenin changed the Russian Empire into the Union of Soviet Socialist Republics (USSR). Lenin, aided by Trotsky (see page 30), the leader of the Red Army, began to transform the country according to his version of communism. However, Lenin died in 1924 and Trotsky was exiled, leaving Joseph Stalin in charge.

## How is this reflected in the novel?

Unlike Lenin, Old Major dies before the Revolution so does not influence what happens on the farm afterwards. The farm, like Russia, is re-named and the new green flag is reminiscent of Lenin's red flag. Trotsky is represented by Snowball, who is both a military leader and a thinker, but is driven out by Napoleon's dogs (equivalent to Stalin's secret police, the NKVD).

## What happened under Stalin?

Stalin acquired more and more power for himself and ruthlessly crushed all opposition. He used **propaganda** to create an **image** of himself as a great, fatherly leader and created the Five-Year Plan to revive the country's industry. At the start of the Second World War he formed an alliance with Hitler, but Germany invaded the USSR in 1941 and the USSR ended the war allied with Britain and the USA.

# How is this reflected in the novel?

Napoleon's use of propaganda is shown in the actions of Squealer. The displaying of Old Major's skull is based on Stalin's display of Lenin's body after his death. The new military orders, ceremonies and parades also reflect Stalin's behaviour. The project to build the windmill is like the Five-Year Plan. The executions in the yard reflect Stalin's 'show trials' and purges. The hens' revolt is based on a 1921 mutiny at a Soviet naval base.

Mr Frederick represents Hitler and the Battle of the Windmill parallels the Battle of Stalingrad (1943). Finally, the card game in Chapter 10 might be seen to parallel the Tehran Conference of 1943 where Stalin, Winston Churchill of Britain and F.D. Roosevelt of the USA met to discuss cooperation between their countries.

## Summary

- There was discontent, poverty and hunger in Russia before the Revolution.
- The Bolsheviks established the USSR and introduced a communist system.
- After Lenin's death, Stalin crushed all opposition.
- Stalin made an alliance with Hitler in 1939, but Hitler invaded the USSR in 1941.

## Questions

QUICK TEST
1. Who was the leader of the Bolsheviks?
2. Who or what do the dogs represent?
3. How do Frederick's actions reflect those of Hitler?

EXAM PRACTICE
Then he put on an extra spurt and, with a few inches to spare, slipped through a hole in the hedge and was seen no more. (Chapter 5)

Relating your ideas to the historical context, write a paragraph explaining how life on Animal Farm reflects events in Russia after the revolution.

# Old Major

**You must be able to:** analyse how Old Major is presented in the novel.

## Who is Old Major?

Old Major is a 12-year-old prize Middle White boar. A boar is a male pig, kept for breeding rather than meat.

## Who does he represent in the allegory?

He is the equivalent of Lenin, the leader of the Bolshevik Party and the Russian Revolution. Unlike Lenin, Old Major dies before the Rebellion.

## What is his function in the novel?

Old Major expresses the grievances of the animals and puts forward the ideas on which the Rebellion is based. After his death, he is revered.

## What is his character?

He appears 'wise and benevolent'. He has developed a political philosophy from experience and observation. He is an **orator**, using **rhetorical devices** to deliver his message. He is democratic: he asks for a vote on whether wild creatures are comrades. He is inspirational.

## What is his message?

Animals work hard during short, miserable lives. This is not just part of nature. Animals' problems are caused by Man. Animals must overthrow Man in order to become rich and free.

## How does Old Major deliver his message?

He engages his audience's interest by mentioning a dream but says he will talk about it later.

Old Major asserts his authority by talking about his long life, which has given him wisdom, and his imminent death.

He uses **rhetorical questions**, for example 'what is the nature of this life of ours?', to include the audience and provoke thought.

He uses repetition to emphasise his points, for example, 'No animal ... no animal ... the life of an animal'.

He uses direct address to show how his message applies to all, for example, 'you hens'. He also gives examples to back up his general point.

He uses **emotive** language to describe the animals' lives and deaths, for example, 'every one of you will scream your lives out'.

He uses **imperatives** to reinforce his authority, for example 'Never listen'.

He uses **simple sentences** to create memorable **slogans**, for example, 'All animals are equal'.

At the end of the speech, he returns to his dream and uses an **anecdote** about his childhood to create a mood that is sentimental and optimistic.

Finally, he uses the song 'Beasts of England' to create excitement and enthusiasm.

## How do the animals react to him?

They respect him and listen attentively to his speech. They react enthusiastically to the song.

After his death, his speech inspires the animals and changes their outlook. The pigs develop his ideas into the system they call Animalism. Later, Napoleon uses Old Major to give himself greater authority, by digging up and displaying his skull.

## Key Quotations to Learn

A majestic looking pig, with a wise and benevolent appearance. (Chapter 1)

'I understand the nature of life on this earth as well as any animal now living.' (Old Major: Chapter 1)

'All men are enemies. All animals are comrades.' (Old Major: Chapter 1)

## Summary

- Old Major is respected by the other animals.
- He gives a speech about the animals' lives and urges them to rebel.
- He uses rhetorical devices to convince the animals.
- After his death, Napoleon uses Old Major to increase his own authority.

## Sample Analysis

Old Major begins by addressing the animals as 'comrades', a term used by socialists to show that speaker and audience are equal and on the same side. He then refers to the 'dream' he had. The word has **connotations** of hopes and ambitions, suggesting that he has an ambition for the future. Later, he describes what he says is an actual dream. Expressing his vision of the future in this way **implies** that Old Major is a visionary and a prophet.

## Questions

QUICK TEST

1. What sort of animal is Old Major?
2. Which Russian leader does he represent?
3. How does Napoleon use Old Major to give him authority?

EXAM PRACTICE

Using at least one of the 'Key Quotations to Learn', write a paragraph explaining how Orwell presents Old Major as an inspirational speaker.

# Napoleon

**You must be able to:** analyse how Napoleon is presented in the novel.

## Who is Napoleon?

Napoleon is a 'large, fierce-looking Berkshire boar' (Chapter 2). From the start, he is one of the leading pigs. He is named after Napoleon Bonaparte (1769–1821), a French military leader who conquered much of Europe and eventually declared himself Emperor.

## Who does he represent in the allegory?

He is the equivalent of Joseph Stalin (1879–1953). Stalin had taken control of the Communist Party by 1927 and remained in power until his death.

## What is his function in the novel?

The novel traces Napoleon's rise to power and through him we see how idealism changes to totalitarianism. Although he is the protagonist, we do not share his thoughts or feelings.

## What is Napoleon's character?

He has a 'reputation for getting his own way' (Chapter 2). He is not interested in debate. He is vain, arrogant, cunning and deceitful but can also be brave and has natural authority.

## How does he show his character through his actions?

At first, Snowball and Napoleon act together but they soon become rivals. A key difference between them is shown in Chapter 3 when Napoleon, instead of getting involved in organisation, takes away the puppies to train. This shows his lust for power and his deceitful nature.

He shows his cunning by keeping back the milk and continues to deceive the animals, for example, in the revised version he gives of Snowball's actions (Chapters 5 and 6) and his lies about his dealings with the farmers. However, he is not as clever as he thinks he is, as shown by the way he is fooled by Frederick in Chapter 8.

When Snowball is expelled (Chapter 5), Napoleon's true nature becomes clear. He is now in control and begins to betray the principles of Animalism, shown by the changes to the Commandments. His corruption is also shown in his gradual adoption of human ways.

His cruelty and ruthlessness become apparent when he directs the executions in the yard (Chapter 7), and continues throughout the novel.

His arrogance and vanity, as well as his increasing power, are shown in his invention of titles for himself and the poem that Minimus writes about him (Chapter 8).

He shows bravery when he is the only animal who remains standing when the windmill is blown up (Chapter 8).

# How do other characters react to Napoleon?

They accept Napoleon as their leader and are deceived by him. Boxer's belief that 'Napoleon is always right' is shared by most of them. Any doubts are overcome by loyalty to Napoleon and Animalism. The few animals who are unconvinced, such as Benjamin, keep quiet.

Napoleon keeps power through a combination of the animals' unquestioning loyalty (and stupidity), deceit and fear.

## Key Quotations to Learn

… not much of a talker but with a reputation for getting his own way. (Chapter 2)

'If Comrade Napoleon says it, it must be right.' (Boxer: Chapter 5)

Napoleon stood sternly surveying his audience; then he uttered a high-pitched whimper. (Chapter 7)

## Summary

- Napoleon is the novel's protagonist.
- He is driven by desire for power.
- He is cunning, deceitful, cruel, ruthless and vain.
- He is admired and feared by the other animals.

## Sample Analysis

In Chapter 8, Napoleon becomes a distant figure, separated from the other animals. The extent of his power is shown by the attendance of the black cockerel (the colour black having connotations of fascism) and the dogs. The dogs 'wait upon him', **implying** they are personal servants and so animals are no longer equal. He and the principles of Animalism have been corrupted by power and wealth. He eats from the Crown Derby dinner service, which would have been used by the humans only on special occasions, so he not only behaves like the Joneses but outdoes them in showy displays of wealth.

## Questions

QUICK TEST
1. Which Russian leader does Napoleon resemble?
2. Who is his rival for power?
3. What aspects of his character are demonstrated when he has a poem written about him?

EXAM PRACTICE
Using at least one of the 'Key Quotations to Learn', write a paragraph explaining how Orwell presents Napoleon's love of power.

# Snowball

**You must be able to:** analyse how Snowball is presented in the novel.

## Who is Snowball?

Snowball is a young boar. After Old Major's death, he and Napoleon become leaders.

## Who does he represent in the allegory?

Snowball is the equivalent of Leon Trotsky (1879–1940), who believed in the need for revolutions across the world. He was the leader of the Red Army. Trotsky was assassinated while in exile in South America.

## What is his function in the novel?

Snowball is Napoleon's **antagonist**. He is the only character who is as strong as Napoleon. He represents an alternative way forward. When he is exiled, there is no-one to oppose Napoleon but Napoleon uses him as a convenient **scapegoat**.

## What is his character?

He is clever, hard-working, practical and brave. He likes to organise things (perhaps to a ridiculous extent), enjoys debate but is not immune to corruption.

## How does he show his character through his actions?

He explains Animalism to the other animals, for example, telling Mollie how to behave in Chapter 2 and in Chapter 3 'proving' to the birds that they have four legs.

He paints the Seven Commandments on the barn wall and there is a sense that, although he and Napoleon are acting together, Snowball is the one who is committed to Animalism.

He organises committees, showing his energy and a love of **bureaucracy**.

He agrees that milk and apples should be reserved for the pigs, showing a degree of corruption.

The Battle of the Cowshed (Chapter 4) demonstrates Snowball's cleverness and his bravery. His tactics, based on his reading of Julius Caesar, are successful. He leads from the front and is injured.

His scheme for the windmill shows his intellectual ability and his ambition for the success of the farm. His **attitude** contrasts with Napoleon's short-sightedness.

Snowball shows his powers of persuasion and leadership when he speaks about the windmill in Chapter 5.

## How do other characters react to Snowball?

The animals are often won over by Snowball's 'brilliant speeches' (Chapter 5) but support is usually divided equally between him and Napoleon.

Napoleon sees Snowball as an enemy. He disagrees with him at meetings, gets the sheep to interrupt him and urinates on his plans. Finally, he sets the dogs on him and drives him from the farm (Chapter 5).

After Snowball has gone, Napoleon lies about him and blames him for everything that goes wrong on the farm. This helps to increase Napoleon's own authority.

Four young pigs who support Snowball are killed. Other animals express concern about the new version of Snowball's history. However, they are persuaded they are wrong and accept Napoleon's version of Snowball's character.

## Key Quotations to Learn

... a more vivacious pig than Napoleon, quicker in speech and more inventive ... (Chapter 2)

... in a moment Snowball's eloquence had carried them away. (Chapter 5)

'Comrades, here and now I pronounce the death sentence upon Snowball.' (Napoleon: Chapter 6)

## Summary

- Snowball is Napoleon's antagonist.
- He is intellectual, energetic and brave.
- After driving him out, Napoleon uses him as a scapegoat.

## Sample Analysis

Snowball, unlike Napoleon, is 'full of plans for innovations and improvements'. These three **nouns** all have positive connotations, connected with the future. Snowball is here portrayed as intellectual, making 'a close study' of farming magazines and 'talking learnedly' about his subject, but the nature of his plans is emphasised by the use of plain, even crude, vocabulary describing the basic concerns of farming: 'field drains, silage and basic slag' and even 'dung'. His plans are not vaguely theoretical or political, but down-to-earth and practical.

## Questions

QUICK TEST
1. Which Russian leader does Snowball resemble?
2. How does the Battle of the Cowshed show Snowball's cleverness?
3. Which animals are killed because of their support for Snowball?

EXAM PRACTICE
Using at least one of the 'Key Quotations to Learn', write a paragraph explaining how Orwell presents Snowball's character.

**Squealer**

**You must be able to:** analyse how Squealer is presented in the novel.

## Who is Squealer?

Squealer is a 'porker', a pig raised for meat.

## Who does he represent?

Squealer represents Stalin's propaganda machine and the Soviet press. In the USSR, all information was controlled by the Communist Party.

## What is his function in the novel?

He helps the pigs, especially Napoleon, to increase and maintain their power by presenting their version of things and persuading the other animals to believe it.

## What is his character?

He has a shrill voice and is a 'brilliant talker'. He skips from side to side when speaking, reflecting the way he 'skips' around the subject. He is **sycophantic** and loyal to Napoleon. He is also sly and cowardly.

## How does he show his character through his actions?

When Snowball paints the commandments on the barn wall in Chapter 2, Squealer holds the ladder, showing his supportive but inferior position.

When the pigs keep the apples in Chapter 3, Squealer is 'sent' to explain to the other animals. His explanation is a master class in propaganda.

He also uses fear to persuade the animals to accept Napoleon's increasing power (Chapter 5). When he explains Napoleon's change of mind over the windmill, he is clearly lying, being described as 'sly'.

His lies become more outrageous. When he talks about Snowball's plotting (Chapter 7) he appears nervous but his description of the Battle of the Cowshed is convincing. We see a reflection of Napoleon's ruthlessness under his 'twinkling' exterior when he gives Boxer an 'ugly look', suggesting that he will report Boxer to Napoleon.

His absence during the Battle of the Windmill suggests that he is cowardly.

In Chapter 9, he shows his suspicious nature and his role as an informer in the way he looks at the animals before denouncing the 'rumour' about Boxer's death.

## How do other characters react to Squealer?

The other pigs say he could turn black into white, suggesting that they admire both his persuasiveness and his dishonesty (Chapter 2).

The other animals are taken in by his certainty, his ability to invent 'graphic' accounts of events, his use of Napoleon's authority and his use of fear.

They have doubts about his honesty when they remember facts that differ from his stories but they cannot express them. Clover sends to him for help after Boxer's fall (Chapter 9), suggesting the animals trust him.

## Key Quotations to Learn

The others said of Squealer that he could turn black to white. (Chapter 2)

... but Squealer spoke so persuasively, and the three dogs who happened to be with him growled so threateningly, that they accepted his explanation without further questions. (Chapter 5)

... his little eyes darted suspicious glances from side to side ... (Chapter 9)

## Summary

- Squealer is in charge of propaganda.
- He helps Napoleon maintain power by lying to the animals.
- He is clever, **eloquent**, sycophantic, sly and cowardly.

## Sample Analysis

When explaining Napoleon's decision to build the windmill, Squealer looks 'very sly', indicating that he is aware that he is about to lie to the animals. He then manages, while deceiving, to praise Napoleon's supposed use of deceit, transforming 'cunning' into a positive **adjective**. His repetition of the phrase 'tactics, comrades, tactics!' both confuses the animals and persuades them, although the reference to the dogs 'who growled so threateningly' suggests that it is not so much Squealer's persuasive powers as this reminder of Napoleon's power that convinces them.

## Questions

QUICK TEST
1. What does Squealer habitually do while speaking?
2. What does he do when Snowball is painting the Commandments on the barn wall?
3. When does Clover send to him for help?

EXAM PRACTICE
Using at least one of the 'Key Quotations to Learn', write a paragraph explaining how Squealer persuades the other animals that 'black is white'.

# Boxer

**You must be able to:** analyse how Boxer is presented in the novel.

## Who is Boxer?

Boxer is a one of the farm's two cart-horses. He is used to pull farm machinery. Boxer represents a section of the proletariat: hard-working, committed to the Rebellion (Russian Revolution) and loyal to Animalism (the Communist Party).

## What is his function in the novel?

He plays an important part in the Rebellion and the animals' achievements. His unquestioning loyalty helps Napoleon. The circumstances of his death show how far the pigs have departed from Old Major's principles.

## What is his character?

He is strong, works hard and has a steady character. He is loyal and obedient but naive and not very intelligent. Although usually gentle, he occasionally uses his strength in a violent way.

## How does he show his character through his actions?

He adopts a personal motto: 'I will work harder' (Chapter 3). Whenever anything goes wrong his answer is to work. His strength and determination are shown in the building of the windmill (Chapter 6).

He shows his loyalty and commitment to the Rebellion when he puts his straw hat on the fire in Chapter 2, sacrificing his own comfort for a principle.

His loyalty to the cause turns into loyalty to Napoleon. He is easily convinced by Squealer's explanations of things and adopts a new motto: 'Comrade Napoleon is always right'.

His uses his strength in the Battle of the Windmill (Chapter 4) and when the dogs attack him in Chapter 7. However, he does not intend to harm, as shown when he regrets injuring the stable boy.

In Chapter 5, he is 'vaguely troubled' at Snowball's expulsion. In Chapter 7, he shows honesty and naivety when he says he does not believe Squealer's tale. In Chapter 8, after the Battle of the Windmill, he asks 'what victory?'

His doubts are overcome by his sense of loyalty but in Chapter 7 they lead to Napoleon setting the dogs on him. However, he continues to believe that Napoleon is always right and that he will be looked after.

## How do other characters react to Boxer?

He is admired by the other animals for his strength and hard work.

After the Battle of the Cowshed, he is awarded the title of 'Animal Hero First Class'.

His loyalty to Napoleon is not returned.

In Chapter 9, Clover and Benjamin show their affection by looking after him. When he is taken away the animals show their feelings for him by chasing after the van and urging him to escape.

## Key Quotations to Learn

... he was not of first rate intelligence, but he was universally respected for his steadiness of character and tremendous powers of work. (Chapter 1)

His answer to every problem, every set back, was 'I will work harder!' – which he had adopted as his personal motto. (Chapter 3)

'If Comrade Napoleon says it, it must be right.' (Boxer: Chapter 5)

## Summary

- Boxer is hard-working and loyal.
- His stupidity and loyalty help Napoleon and the pigs.
- He is admired and loved by the other animals.

## Sample Analysis

Boxer is known for his commitment to the Rebellion so when 'Even Boxer was vaguely troubled' after Snowball's departure, it is an indication of how much potential opposition there is to Napoleon. However, Squealer appeals to 'Loyalty and obedience' and 'discipline', concepts that the animals rejected by rebelling against Jones. The ease with which Boxer accepts this when he voices 'the general feeling' suggests that he wants to be told what to do and what to think and is **complicit** in the development of Napoleon's totalitarianism.

## Questions

QUICK TEST
1. What is Boxer's first motto?
2. In Boxer's view, who is always right?
3. Where is he taken at the end of the novel?

EXAM PRACTICE
Using at least one of the 'Key Quotations to Learn', write a paragraph explaining how Orwell presents the character of Boxer.

# Clover and Mollie

**You must be able to:** analyse how Clover and Mollie are presented in the novel.

## Who are Clover and Mollie?

Clover is a one of the farm's two cart-horses. Mollie is the horse who pulls Mrs Jones's trap (a small carriage).

## What is Clover's function in the novel?

She is the female equivalent of Boxer, her commitment and loyalty being essential to the animals' success.

## What is Clover's character?

She is strong but gentle, motherly, loyal and hard-working. She is sensitive and a bit more intelligent than Boxer.

## How does Clover show her character through her actions?

In Chapter 1, she uses her strength to protect the motherless ducklings. She shows her commitment and loyalty, as well as her motherly side, by confronting Mollie about her behaviour in Chapter 5.

The difference between her and Boxer is shown in Chapter 6 when he accepts that the pigs are sleeping in beds but she remembers it is forbidden and asks Muriel to read the relevant commandment to her.

Her concern grows after the executions. Nevertheless, she accepts that things are better than they were and 'she would remain faithful' (Chapter 7).

In Chapter 9, she looks after Boxer, showing love and loyalty, and also her trusting nature when she sends for Squealer. At the end of the novel, she continues to teach new animals about Animalism (Chapter 10).

## What is Mollie's function in the novel?

She represents those who have no interest in Revolution or change, being happy with her own life and unconcerned about others.

## What is Mollie's character?

She is foolish, selfish, vain, lazy and cowardly but independent.

## How does Mollie show her character through her actions?

In Chapter 2, she asks 'the stupidest questions' and is found admiring herself in a mirror.

She gets up late and leaves work early (Chapter 3). She disappears during the Battle of the Cowshed and is found hiding in her stall (Chapter 4).

In Chapter 5, Clover sees her with a man from Foxwood and finds sugar and ribbons hidden in her stall. Soon afterwards she disappears.

## Key Quotations to Learn

[Clover was] a stout motherly mare approaching middle life ... (Chapter 1)

Mollie, the foolish, pretty white mare [...] came mincing daintily in, chewing at a lump of sugar. (Chapter 1)

But still, it was not for this that she [Clover] and all the other animals had hoped and toiled. (Chapter 7)

## Summary

- Clover is motherly, loyal and caring.
- She has doubts but remains faithful to Animalism.
- Mollie is self-centred and prefers life with human beings.

## Sample Analysis

In Chapter 7, Orwell uses Clover to explore the difference between the ideals of the Rebellion and the reality of life. Using **free indirect discourse**, he shares her thoughts and feelings with readers. Her simple idealism is based on ideas of fairness and kindness: a society 'free of hunger and the whip' and 'the strong protecting the weak'. Her memory of protecting the ducklings in the barn illustrates how such a society should work in practice. Her realisation that her principles have been betrayed is touching and sad but it is also frustrating as she re-affirms that 'she would remain faithful', showing how idealistic, well-meaning people can find themselves supporting cruelty and **despotism**.

## Questions

QUICK TEST
1. Who does Clover look after in the barn?
2. What does Mollie hide in her stall?
3. Who confronts Mollie about her behaviour?

EXAM PRACTICE
Using at least one of the 'Key Quotations to Learn', write a paragraph explaining how Orwell presents Clover's feelings about changes on Animal Farm.

# Benjamin, Muriel and Moses

**You must be able to:** analyse how Benjamin and Muriel are presented in the novel.

## Who are Benjamin, Muriel and Moses?

Benjamin is an old donkey. Muriel is a goat. Moses is a pet raven.

## What is their function in the novel?

Benjamin sometimes gives a cynical view of what is happening. He can be seen as an intellectual who keeps out of politics. Muriel reads the altered commandments to Clover, alerting her and the reader to the betrayal of the principles of Animalism. Moses represents religion.

## What is Benjamin's character?

He is intelligent but cynical and bad-tempered. He is 'devoted to Boxer' (Chapter 1). He could be seen as selfish in his refusal to get involved.

## How does Benjamin show his character through his actions?

After the Rebellion, he works 'in the same slow obstinate way' as he did before. He does not express an opinion about what is happening (Chapter 2).

He learns to read as well as the pigs but says there is nothing worth reading (Chapter 3).

In Chapter 8, he refuses to read the Commandments to Clover because he does not want to 'meddle'. His refusal to meddle contributes to Napoleon's success. Later, he watches the men preparing to blow up the windmill with 'an air almost of amusement'.

In Chapter 9, he shows his feelings towards Boxer by looking after him after his fall and finally takes an active part in events when he reads the writing on the side of the van that is taking Boxer away.

## What is Muriel's character?

She is more intelligent than most of the animals. She is helpful.

## How does Muriel show her character through her actions?

She learns to read well, although not as well as Benjamin. Unlike him, she makes use of her skills by reading to the other animals (Chapter 3).

In Chapters 6 and 8 she reads the altered Commandments but she does not make any comment on what is happening.

## What is Moses' character?

He is 'tame', closer to the humans than the other animals. He is a spy and a tale-bearer but a good talker, who tells tales about Sugarcandy Mountain in the sky (Chapter 2).

# How does Moses show his character through his actions?

In Chapter 2, he follows Mrs Jones off the farm, choosing to be a pet rather than a free animal.

He returns to the farm in Chapter 9. Some of the animals believe his stories and the pigs say he is lying but encourage him to stay.

## Key Quotations to Learn

... without openly admitting it, he [Benjamin] was devoted to Boxer ... (Chapter 1)

'Donkeys live a long time. None of you has ever seen a dead donkey,' (Benjamin: Chapter 3)

'Fools! Fools!' shouted Benjamin [...] 'Do you not see what is written on the side of that van?' (Chapter 9)

## Summary

- Benjamin is intelligent but cynical, and refuses to meddle.
- He is devoted to Boxer and looks after him.
- Muriel reads the altered Commandments to Clover.
- Moses tells the animals about Sugarcandy Mountain.

## Sample Analysis

Benjamin shows his deep affection for Boxer as he is described 'galloping' and 'braying at the top of his voice' in a state of excitement no-one has ever seen before when the knacker's van comes to take Boxer away. However, he also shows his contempt for the other animals by addressing them as 'Fools!'. When he pushes Muriel aside to read the words on the van, the reader might recall his previous refusal to 'meddle' and read the Commandments to Clover. If he had used his intelligence to 'meddle' earlier, he might not have had to watch his friend being taken to the knacker's yard.

## Questions

QUICK TEST
1. Why, according to Benjamin, does he not read?
2. What does he watch with an air of amusement?
3. Why does he call the other animals 'fools'?

EXAM PRACTICE
Using at least one of the 'Key Quotations to Learn', write a paragraph explaining how Orwell presents the character of Benjamin.

# Other Animals

**You must be able to:** analyse how animals are presented in the novel.

## Which other animals are featured in the novel?

Among the animals Orwell mentions are pigs, dogs, sheep, hens, cows and a cat.

## What is their function in the novel?

They represent different attitudes to the Rebellion and life on *Animal Farm*, reflecting different sections of society in Russia.

## What do the pigs do?

The pigs are the cleverest animals and lead the Rebellion. They control the other animals and gradually become indistinguishable from human beings. They are similar to the **Politburo**, the ruling body of the Communist Party in the USSR.

Four 'young porkers' support Snowball and try to protest about Napoleon's actions but are killed. A pig called Minimus becomes close to Napoleon and writes poems in his honour. The sows (female pigs) have litters sired by Napoleon; his favourite sow dresses in Mrs Jones's clothes.

## What do the dogs do?

The dogs are more intelligent than most animals and learn to read. Two of them, Jessie and Bluebell, have litters of puppies that are taken away to be trained by Napoleon. He turns them into loyal, vicious bodyguards. They chase Snowball from the farm, kill on Napoleon's orders and strike fear in the other animals. They are the equivalent of Lenin's secret police, the NKVD.

## What do the sheep do?

The sheep are stupid and easily led, as sheep are traditionally depicted. They are loyal to Napoleon and the pigs and are used to drown out opposition with their bleating/chanting. In this they are like members of Stalin's Communist Party.

## What are the hens like?

The hens play a major part in Chapter 7 when they rebel against Napoleon's plan to sell their eggs. Their rebellion is soon put down in a way that shows Napoleon's increasing ruthlessness. Their rebellion is similar to a mutiny at a Russian naval base in 1921.

## What do the cows do?

One of the cows kicks in the store shed door at the start of the Rebellion. The pigs' action in taking their milk is the first sign of the pigs becoming corrupt.

## What does the cat do?

As little as possible! She sleeps through Old Major's speech and comes and goes as she pleases. In Chapter 3 she joins Snowball's 'Re-education Committee' in an unsuccessful attempt to 'make friends' with the birds.

## Key Quotations to Learn

... the sheep had taken to bleating 'Four legs good, two legs bad' both in and out of season, and they often interrupted the Meeting with this. (Chapter 5)

Though not yet full-grown they were huge dogs, and as fierce-looking as wolves. (Chapter 5)

... the hens made a determined effort to thwart Napoleon's wishes. (Chapter 7)

## Summary

- Different animals represent different attitudes to the Rebellion.
- The dogs trained by Napoleon become his bodyguards and are like the NKVD.
- The sheep are used to drown out opposition.
- The hens' rebellion is ruthlessly crushed.

## Sample Analysis

Many of the animals have the stereotypical characteristics of their kind, which Orwell makes use of to equate them with different types of people, as in a fable. The sheep, for example, are stupid, easily led and have a 'flock' mentality. Their 'bleating' becomes 'chanting' of the sort heard at political rallies. They are the kind of supporters a leader like Napoleon can rely on to follow him without question and prevent others being heard.

## Questions

QUICK TEST
1. Who is Minimus?
2. What happens to Jessie and Bluebell's puppies?
3. What does a cow do to start the Rebellion?

EXAM PRACTICE
Using at least one of the 'Key Quotations to Learn', write a paragraph explaining how Orwell presents either the dogs or the hens.

**The Humans**

**You must be able to:** analyse how human beings are presented in the novel.

## Which human beings are featured in the novel?

Manor Farm is owned by Mr Jones. Mr Pilkington and Mr Frederick own the neighbouring farms. Napoleon deals with the outside world though a solicitor, Mr Whymper.

## Who do they represent in the allegory?

Jones represents Tsar Nicholas II of Russia. Frederick represents Adolf Hitler, Chancellor of Germany. Pilkington represents the more traditional Western powers. At the end, he and his fellow farmers are the equivalent of Britain and the USA.

## What is their function in the novel?

Jones's neglect provides the impetus for the Rebellion. His possible return is used as a threat by the pigs to control the animals.

According to Old Major, humans are 'the enemy'.

Napoleon's dealings with humans show his betrayal of Animalist principles, although it is clear that the farm cannot thrive if he does not deal with them.

In the final chapter, their visit demonstrates how far the pigs have changed and how the animals are no better off than under Jones.

## What does Jones do?

His actions as a farmer are normal but are cruel from the animals' point of view. His drunken neglect of his duties causes the animals finally to rebel. After failing to take back the farm, he eventually retires to another part of the country.

## What does Frederick do?

Frederick owns Pinchfield Farm. He is 'tough' and 'shrewd'. The animals do not want to deal with him when they hear rumours of his cruelty, and are surprised when Napoleon sells the timber to him. He pays for the timber in forged banknotes. His men invade the farm and blow up the windmill, before being driven off by the animals. These events reflect Hitler's invasion of Russia.

## What does Pilkington do?

He owns Foxwood Farm. He is 'easy-going' and the farm is neglected. He does not get on with Frederick. Napoleon announces his intention to sell the timber to him but changes his mind. In Chapter 10, he is shown round the farm and makes a speech praising its achievements and regretting previous 'misunderstandings'.

# What does Whymper do?

He is a solicitor, hired by Napoleon to help him deal with humans. His arrival means that the pigs have broken the principle of not dealing with humans. Napoleon uses him to fool the outside world into thinking the farm is not short of food. It is he who tells Napoleon that Frederick's banknotes are forged.

## Key Quotations to Learn

Some of the animals talked of the duty of loyalty to Mr Jones, whom they referred to as 'Master' ... (Chapter 3)

Its owner, Mr Pilkington, was an easy-going gentleman-farmer ... (Chapter 4)

... terrible stories were leaking out from Pinchfield about the cruelties that Frederick practised upon his animals. (Chapter 8)

## Summary

- According to Animalism, humans are the enemy and animals should not deal with them.
- Napoleon breaks this principle by hiring Whymper and dealing with the farmers.
- Frederick cons Napoleon and invades the farm.

## Sample Analysis

Orwell uses emotive language to create a picture of Frederick's cruelty. It is reported that he 'flogged' a horse to death, 'starved' his cows and killed a dog by 'throwing it into the furnace'. These images would resonate with Orwell's readers, who would have been learning about Hitler's inhuman treatment of Jews and others. This is reflected in the animals' reaction; their 'blood boiled with rage', contrasting with Squealer's advice to 'avoid rash actions'.

## Questions

QUICK TEST
1. What does Jones's drunkenness cause him to do?
2. What are Pilkington's and Frederick's farms called?
3. What is Whymper's profession?

EXAM PRACTICE
Using at least one of the 'Key Quotations to Learn', write a paragraph explaining how Orwell presents human beings in *Animal Farm*.

# Power and Oppression

**You must be able to:** analyse how the themes of power and oppression are presented in the novel.

## What is oppression?

To 'oppress' means to govern tyrannically, treat harshly or unjustly, or to weigh down.

## Who has power in *Animal Farm*?

Mr Jones has absolute power over the animals on Manor Farm. After the Rebellion, the animals have power over the farm. However, as the novel progresses, the pigs take power for themselves. Pilkington and Frederick have power on their own farms.

## Who is oppressed?

According to Animalism, all animals are oppressed by humans. By the end of the novel most of the animals are oppressed by Napoleon and the pigs.

## How are human power and oppression presented in *Animal Farm*?

Old Major explains that Man is the least productive of the animals yet has the most power. He gives examples of how animals are oppressed.

Jones has power but does not exercise it responsibly, drinking instead of feeding the animals.

The animals destroy the symbols of their oppression including chains, knives, reins, harnesses and whips (Chapter 2).

Frederick's oppression is extreme. Rumours of cruel practices emerge from his farm.

## How is the animals' power presented?

The barn becomes a symbol of democracy and the animals' power. However, most of the animals are unable or unwilling to exercise power, allowing the pigs to dominate the meetings.

The pigs gradually acquire power. The others accept the way they take on the management of the farm because they are more suited to brain work than manual labour.

## How is Napoleon able to become so powerful?

He plans for power from the start, when he hides away the puppies. If anyone opposes him, he gets rid of them.

The other animals allow him to acquire power and accept his authority. Most of them are too stupid and trusting to see what he is doing (like Boxer) and/or too frightened to oppose him. The only animal as intelligent as the pigs, Benjamin, refuses to 'meddle'. They are all responsible for what happens on Animal Farm after the Rebellion.

## Key Quotations to Learn

'... he [Man] is Lord of all the animals.' (Old Major: Chapter 1)

The other animals understood how to vote, but could never think of any resolutions of their own. (Chapter 3)

'Do not imagine, comrades, that leadership is a pleasure! On the contrary, it is a deep and heavy responsibility.' (Squealer: Chapter 5)

## Summary

- Old Major explains how humans oppress animals.
- The animals gain power through the Rebellion but most cannot use it.
- The other animals do nothing to stop Napoleon acquiring power.

## Sample Analysis

Orwell presents the reader with powerful imagery of human power over animals when they destroy the **symbols** of Jones's 'hated reign' and their oppression. There are two long sentences giving lists of equipment used to control animals. Each contains only one adjective: 'cruel' in the first, before an elaboration of the use to which the knives were put, and 'degrading' in the second. They are followed by a minor sentence – 'So were the whips' – emphasising the symbolic importance of the whip, a weapon that Jones used to try to stop the Rebellion and one that Napoleon will later appear with.

## Questions

QUICK TEST
1. Name three symbols of the animals' oppression.
2. What does Jones use to assert his power during the Rebellion?
3. How does Benjamin help Napoleon to acquire power?

EXAM PRACTICE
Using at least one of the 'Key Quotations to Learn', write a paragraph explaining how the power of the pigs is presented in *Animal Farm*.

# Freedom and Equality

**You must be able to:** analyse how the themes of freedom and equality are presented in the novel.

## What does Old Major say about freedom and equality?

Old Major speaks about animals working for themselves, not being treated cruelly and living until their lives naturally end. The only way to achieve freedom is through rebellion.

His vision of freedom is expressed in the words of 'Beasts of England'. The song paints a picture of a **pastoral idyll** with no humans.

He says that 'all animals are equal' but he does not explain how equality can be achieved.

He suggests that they are not inherently equal when he says they are brothers whether 'weak or strong, clever or simple'.

## How does Orwell explore ideas about freedom after the Rebellion?

The animals celebrate their freedom by destroying the symbols of their oppression, such as harnesses and whips, and by running around the farm. The paragraph that describes this is reminiscent of Old Major's idealised vision of **rural** life (Chapter 2).

The Seven Commandments remind us that freedom cannot be absolute. The animals live by rules and therefore have limits on their freedom. Most of them accept this. Mollie, however, is not free to live the life she wants and leaves the farm. She chooses 'slavery' over freedom.

Awareness of their freedom changes their attitude. They work willingly and are happy. They have more to eat and more leisure time.

As Napoleon acquires power, the animals have less freedom. He abolishes the meetings, so they cannot express their views. Everything is done under his orders.

By the end of the novel, there is little real freedom but it is still a powerful concept as animals such as Clover cling to the idea that anything is better than the return of Jones (Chapter 7). This helps Napoleon to control the other animals.

## How does Orwell explore ideas about equality?

The description of the harvest in Chapter 3 shows a society working to the socialist principles of everyone contributing according to their ability and benefitting according to their needs. Because they are equal, nobody steals or quarrels.

However, the pigs do not work, but supervise and direct. Orwell ironically suggests that it is 'natural' for them to lead because of their 'superior knowledge'.

Another sign of the erosion of equality comes when the pigs keep the apples for themselves. They gradually acquire more privileges until they change the Seventh Commandment to the nonsensical 'All animals are equal but some animals are more equal than others'.

Some readers might conclude that Orwell is saying that true equality is impossible: either because some are naturally superior to others or because there will always be some who, driven by greed or ambition, want to have more than others.

Others might see his description of the harvest as a vision of what is possible and the rest of the novel as a warning about how ideals can be destroyed.

## Key Quotations to Learn

'Weak or strong, clever or simple, we are all brothers.' (Old Major: Chapter 1)

Besides, in those days they had been slaves and now they were free, and that made all the difference, as Squealer did not fail to point out. (Chapter 9)

ALL ANIMALS ARE EQUAL BUT SOME ANIMALS ARE MORE EQUAL THAN OTHERS (Chapter 10)

## Summary

- Old Major has a vision of all animals being free and equal.
- As the novel progresses, the animals have less freedom and equality.
- Freedom and equality may be impossible to achieve.

## Sample Analysis

There is irony in Mollie and Snowball's conversation about whether she will 'be allowed' to wear ribbons in her mane, both in her question, as she clearly does not feel free to make decisions, and in Snowball's answer that ribbons are 'the badge of slavery'. Snowball adds to the list of symbols of slavery something which is not in itself harmful or cruel, like the whips, or even used to physically control, like harnesses. This indicates that 'liberty' will be interpreted by the pigs and limited by their rules.

## Questions

QUICK TEST
1. According to Old Major, how can animals achieve freedom?
2. Which Commandment states that all animals are equal?
3. Which character prefers slavery to freedom?

EXAM PRACTICE
Using at least one of the 'Key Quotations to Learn', write a paragraph explaining how the idea of equality is presented in *Animal Farm*.

# Corruption

**You must be able to:** analyse how the theme of corruption is presented in the novel.

## What is corruption?

Corruption literally means decomposition or becoming rotten. In this context, it refers to moral deterioration. Corruption is often associated with greed.

## Who is corrupt in *Animal Farm*?

The pigs become corrupted as the novel progresses. The human farmers are also corrupt. Mollie and Moses are corrupted in different ways.

## How does Orwell explore ideas about corruption?

It has been said that power corrupts and absolute power corrupts absolutely. Love of power, coupled with greed and **materialism**, corrupts the pigs.

The first sign that they are becoming corrupted comes when they keep the apples and milk (Chapter 3). Their greed makes them act against the principle of equality and lie about their actions to the other animals. Snowball, the pig who is apparently most keen on the principles of Animalism, agrees with this action.

They continue to be lured into breaking the Commandments by the material attractions of human life: eating at the table, sleeping in the beds, drinking alcohol and wearing clothes.

Napoleon's desire for money leads to moral corruption when he decides to sell the timber to Frederick despite his cruelty.

Napoleon has already abandoned the principle of not dealing with the humans ('the enemy') in order to sell farm produce to them, an action which leaves the other animals close to starvation while the pigs thrive.

Frederick and Pilkington are also shown to be corrupt as they abandon their objections to Animal Farm when they see they can benefit from dealing with the animals.

Mollie is corrupted in a very simple way when a man gives her sugar and ribbons, causing her to leave the farm. The process by which the pigs are corrupted is more subtle and complicated but also more calculated and harmful to others.

Moses, the raven who was the farmer's pet, returns to the farm after a long absence and is rewarded by the pigs. This suggests the corruption of the **Russian Orthodox Church**.

## Key Quotations to Learn

'It is for your *sake* that we drink that milk and eat those apples,' (Squealer: Chapter 3)

It was also more suited to the dignity of the Leader [...] to live in a house than in a mere sty. (Chapter 6)

Napoleon reposed on a bed of straw on the platform, with the money at his side, neatly piled on a china dish from the farmhouse kitchen. (Chapter 8)

## Summary

- The pigs are corrupted by greed and power.
- This causes them to break the Commandments and the principles of Animalism.
- Mollie, Moses and the humans also provide examples of corruption.

## Sample Analysis

Napoleon's drunkenness and subsequent hangover are absurdly comic, using humour to show how much like Jones he has become, even wearing his 'old bowler hat' as he gallops around the yard. Readers will recall that it was Jones's drunkenness that caused him to neglect the farm. Now Napoleon too has been corrupted by alcohol, ignoring the Fifth Commandment. By ploughing up the paddock, he demonstrates selfishness and a lack of concern for his 'comrades': it had been set aside to be used by 'animals who were past work'.

## Questions

QUICK TEST
1. What corrupts the pigs?
2. How do they show their greed in Chapter 3?
3. Which two animals, apart from the pigs, can be said to be corrupt?

EXAM PRACTICE
Using at least one of the 'Key Quotations to Learn', write a paragraph explaining how the idea of corruption is presented in *Animal Farm*.

**You must be able to:** analyse how the theme of violence is presented in the novel.

## What does Old Major say about violence?

Old Major describes Man's violence towards animals. He stops the dogs from chasing the rats. He says that no animal should ever kill another animal.

He does not specifically condone violence against humans but his call for the animals to rebel against the 'enemy' implies that this is acceptable.

## How does Orwell describe the battles?

In the battles, humans are the aggressors. Readers are likely to be sympathetic to the animals because they are defending themselves against a stronger enemy.

In Chapter 2, sympathy for the animals is increased by the description of Jones's drunkenness and neglect. The hungry animals are justified in breaking into the store. It is the aggressive response of Jones that starts the violence.

In Chapter 4, armed men are again the aggressors as they invade the farm.

Orwell's description of the battle is both exciting and comic, from the 'terrifying spectacle' of Boxer rearing up to the geese pecking at the men's calves.

Boxer's concern about the injured stable boy suggests that the animals are not naturally violent. Snowball's assertion that 'war is war' implies that their violence is justified.

At the Battle of the Windmill (Chapter 8), the level of violence is increased and its effects are more serious. Orwell focusses on the animals' 'courage' and unity. The men, in contrast, are 'contemptible' and 'cruel'.

The battles are all followed by talk of heroism and bravery, but there is a change of tone after the Battle of the Windmill. The animals' triumph is tempered by their losses. However, the celebrations are greater than ever, giving a sense of war being glorified and used to distract the animals from their problems.

## How is Napoleon's violence portrayed?

Napoleon is the only animal to use violence against another animal. Unlike the acts of war, his actions, except at the Battle of the Windmill, are neither justified nor brave.

Orwell builds a sense of Napoleon's increasing cruelty. In Chapter 5, the dogs are aggressive but no-one is hurt. In Chapter 7, nine hens die after opposing Napoleon, but their death is not described. Later in the same chapter, Orwell gives a full and bloody description of the executions in the yard. It ends with a pile of corpses and a smell of blood 'unknown there since the expulsion of Jones'.

This shows that Napoleon is now no better than Jones or Frederick, whose cruelty is described in Chapter 8. When Napoleon sends Boxer to the knacker's, readers might recall Old Major's description of what happens there in Chapter 1.

## Key Quotations to Learn

'No animal must ever kill any other animal.' (Old Major: Chapter 1)

'No sentimentality, comrade!' cried Snowball, from whose wounds the blood was still dripping. 'War is war. The only good human being is a dead one.' (Chapter 4)

... the air was heavy with the smell of blood, which had been unknown there since the expulsion of Jones. (Chapter 7)

## Summary

- The animals use violence to defend themselves against human beings.
- Orwell creates sympathy for the animals and makes the battles tense and exciting.
- Napoleon uses violence against other animals and breaks the Sixth Commandment.

## Sample Analysis

After the excitement of the Battle of the Cowshed, the mood changes. Boxer is 'pawing with his hoof at the stable-lad'. The **verb** 'pawing' describes a gentle action, natural for a horse. It is significant that his victim is a 'stable-lad', whose job would have been to look after the horses, rather than a powerful farmer. Boxer is reprimanded by Snowball, who asserts that 'the only good human being is a dead one'. His attitude brings home the reality of revolution: violence is necessary and there is no room for 'sentimentality'.

## Questions

QUICK TEST
1. What does Old Major stop the dogs doing?
2. What can be inferred from Boxer's concern for the stable boy?
3. Which two of these words describe the animals during the Battle of the Windmill: courageous, cruel, cowardly, unified?

EXAM PRACTICE
Using at least one of the 'Key Quotations to Learn', write a paragraph explaining how Orwell presents violent conflict in one of the battles in *Animal Farm*.

# Deceit and Propaganda

**You must be able to:** analyse how the themes of deceit and propaganda are presented in the novel.

## What is propaganda?

Propaganda means the spread of information and/or ideas, usually by governments or political parties. Propaganda is always one-sided and sometimes false.

## How are deceit and propaganda presented?

The pigs use the pigeons to spread propaganda about Animal Farm to other farms. This achieves some success in causing other animals to rebel. The propaganda they spread, through Squealer, on Animal Farm is designed to present the pigs in a good light and is usually false.

When Napoleon and Squealer deceive the other animals, we are not told that they are lying. Orwell reports what they do without comment and gives the other animals' reactions. Readers can see what is going on but the animals cannot.

After Snowball's expulsion, Squealer claims that Napoleon designed the windmill. There is a hint that he is lying in the 'sly look' he gives the animals.

They invent ever more fantastic lies about Snowball, even though the other animals remember the truth. Some animals 'confess' to plotting with Snowball. They have moved from passive acceptance of the pigs' deceit to taking part in it – even though they pay for it with their lives.

Squealer uses false statistics to deceive the animals into thinking the farm is successful. Squealer also lies about Boxer's death. The animals believe his story despite what they saw with their own eyes.

Perhaps the biggest deceit is the alteration of the Seven Commandments. This demonstrates their betrayal of the principles of the Rebellion.

A final example of deceit comes in the last chapter when Napoleon and Pilkington both put down the same card. One of them is cheating. It does not matter which one. The message is that the pigs have become as dishonest as humans.

## Is deceit always a bad thing?

Snowball deceives the enemy at the Battle of the Cowshed. He uses deceit for the good of his comrades and against their enemy.

Squealer gives Napoleon's 'tactics' as an explanation for his change of mind over the windmill, implying this is morally acceptable as the result is in their interest – although in this case, Squealer is deceiving them about Napoleon's deceit!

Napoleon fools Whymper into thinking the animals have plenty of food, but he is motivated by self-interest, not the common good.

## Key Quotations to Learn

This, said Squealer, was something called tactics. (Chapter 5)

'Comrades,' he said quietly, 'do you know who is responsible for this? Do you know the enemy who has come in the night and overthrown our windmill? SNOWBALL!' (Napoleon: Chapter 6)

Squealer came to announce the news to the others. He had, he said, been present during Boxer's last hours. (Chapter 9)

## Summary

- The pigs' lies become bolder and more elaborate as the novel progresses.
- Napoleon and Squealer lie about Snowball.
- The other animals do not challenge the lies.

## Sample Analysis

Squealer presents himself as a first-hand witness, 'present during Boxer's last hours'. He reinforces his tale by manipulating the animals' emotions. He calls it the 'most affecting sight' he has seen and wipes away a tear. As ever, he seeks to make his lie convincing with a mixture of emotion and detail. His account of Boxer's 'last words' cleverly uses Boxer's 'motto' ('Napoleon is always right') to appeal to the animals' loyalty to Animal Farm and their affection for Boxer.

## Questions

QUICK TEST
1. What does Napoleon do in Chapter 2 that gives us a hint of his deceit?
2. Who really designed the windmill?
3. When does Snowball practise deceit for the good of the farm?

EXAM PRACTICE
Using at least one of the 'Key Quotations to Learn', write a paragraph explaining how the theme of deceit is presented in *Animal Farm*.

# Religion and Ritual

**You must be able to:** analyse how religion and ritual are presented in the novel.

## How does Moses represent religion?

Moses is black, recalling the robes worn by priests of many religions, including the Russian Orthodox Church.

Many people in Russia associated the church with the royal family and the **aristocracy**, and thought that it was corrupt.

Moses is a spy and a 'tale-bearer'. He also tells stories about a place called 'Sugarcandy Mountain', which animals go to when they die. This represents the Christian idea of Heaven.

When Moses leaves with the humans, he shows which side he is on.

## What is the pigs' attitude to Moses?

In Chapter 2, the pigs convince the other animals that there is no such place as Sugarcandy Mountain.

However, when Moses returns in Chapter 9, the pigs let him stay and give him an allowance of beer. This demonstrates their **hypocrisy** and betrayal of Animalism. Now that things are not going well, the hope of a happy afterlife can help keep the animals docile. Religion has become another way of controlling the workers.

The Seven Commandments reference the Ten Commandments, the basis of Jewish and Christian morality. Animalism can be seen as an alternative to religion.

## What is ritual?

'Ritual' refers to ordered ceremonies, usually associated with religion. Most countries have rituals and ceremonies involving religion and/or the armed forces.

## How is ritual presented in *Animal Farm*?

After the Rebellion, the animals immediately start to use ritual. The flag is hoisted in the garden and the meeting ends with the singing of 'Beasts of England'. This shows the animals forging an identity for Animal Farm. Flags and **anthems** are powerful symbols of identity for nations and for political parties.

Later, Napoleon adds more ritual. The animals march past the flag, the gun and Old Major's skull, three reminders of their history and identity.

Ceremonies take place to award honours, initially to deserving recipients like Snowball and Boxer but later to Napoleon. Napoleon's medals and the replacement of 'Beasts of England' with a song in his honour show him using ritual as a means of control. This reflects the 'cult of personality' that is often attached to totalitarian leaders.

On the farm, ritual is used to keep the animals happy and distracted. **Secular** ritual fulfils the same function as religious ritual.

## Key Quotations to Learn

Some of them believed in Sugarcandy Mountain, and the pigs had to argue very hard to convince them that there was no such place. (Chapter 2)

They all declared contemptuously that his stories about Sugarcandy Mountain were lies, and yet they allowed him to remain on the farm, not working, with an allowance of a gill of beer a day. (Chapter 9)

So that with the songs, the processions, Squealer's lists of figures, the thunder of the gun, the crowing of the cockerel and the fluttering of the flag, they were able to forget that their bellies were empty. (Chapter 9)

## Summary

- Religion is represented by Moses.
- The pigs do not believe in Sugarcandy Mountain but encourage Moses to stay.
- Ritual is used to create a sense of identity and to control.

## Sample Analysis

Sugarcandy Mountain, according to Moses, is 'somewhere up in the sky', recalling childish ideas of the Christian Heaven. He promises the animals it is 'Sunday seven days a week' there, they will get clover all the year round and sugar grows on hedges. This idea attracts some animals despite its absurdity, implying that religion is both ridiculous and designed for the **gullible**. However, it is not that different from Old Major's vision of a future England, expressed in 'Beasts of England', with its promise of 'riches more than mind can picture' in 'the golden future time'.

## Questions

QUICK TEST
1. Where does Moses say animals go when they die?
2. How do the pigs show their hypocrisy in Chapter 9?
3. What are the first two rituals the animals adopt?

EXAM PRACTICE
Using at least one of the 'Key Quotations to Learn', write a paragraph explaining how religion is presented in *Animal Farm*.

# Language

You must be able to: analyse how ideas about language are presented in the novel.

## Why is language important in the novel?

Orwell was interested in and concerned about the way language can be changed and manipulated for political purposes.

## How are ideas about language presented in the novel?

Being able to use language well gives power and influence.

Old Major's skill with language is essential to getting his message across. He is portrayed as an orator, using rhetorical techniques to influence his audience.

Three other characters are said to be good talkers: Snowball, Squealer and Moses. Snowball uses his skills to explain and develop the ideas of Animalism; Squealer can 'turn black into white' and uses language to deceive; Moses uses his skills to tell tales.

The pigs realise the importance of being able to use written as well as spoken language. They teach themselves to read and write before the Rebellion, and afterwards they try to teach the other animals.

Orwell uses the animals' language skills as an indicator of their intelligence. Benjamin is the only animal that can read as well as the pigs. Muriel and the dogs can also read well. Clover learns the alphabet, while Boxer and Mollie each learn a few letters. No-one else gets beyond the letter A.

Language skills give the pigs access to knowledge, as when they read about farming and war, and their superior knowledge makes their argument that only they can manage the farm plausible.

Apart from telling outright lies, the pigs distort the **rhetoric** of the revolution. The word 'comrade', used to denote equality, loses its meaning when Napoleon is called by the **oxymoronic** title 'our Leader, Comrade Napoleon' (Chapter 7).

Squealer, explaining how the pigs can sleep in beds, changes the meaning of the word 'bed'. Snowball redefines 'legs' for the benefit of the birds. Snowball's slogan 'Four legs good, two legs bad' is changed by one word so that it comes to mean the opposite of the original. They proclaim extra work and processions are 'voluntary' when they are actually compulsory. They use **euphemisms** to make things sound better. Finally, they replace the Commandments with a slogan that makes no sense at all: it is impossible to be more equal or less equal.

They change language to justify their behaviour and maintain their power.

## Key Quotations to Learn

The birds did not understand Snowball's long words, but they accepted his explanation. (Chapter 3)

'... he would have succeeded if it had not been for our heroic Leader, Comrade Napoleon.' (Squealer: Chapter 7)

For the time being, certainly, it had been found necessary to make a readjustment of rations (Squealer always spoke of it as a 'readjustment', never as a 'reduction'), (Chapter 9)

## Summary

- Language skills give power and influence.
- The animals' ability to read and write reflects their degrees of intelligence.
- The pigs distort language to justify their behaviour.

## Sample Analysis

Hearing Clover's concerns about the change to the Fourth Commandment, Squealer asks three rhetorical questions in quick succession, not giving the others a chance to answer. He justifies the pigs' use of beds by re-defining the word 'bed' to include anywhere that an animal might sleep. Like Snowball's earlier re-definition of 'legs', his argument is logical and convincing, although clearly nonsensical. He ends his speech with another series of three rhetorical questions, building to the ultimate question: 'Surely none of you wishes to have Jones back?' He has used rhetoric and distortion of language to successfully argue that the pigs sleeping in beds will stop the return of Jones.

## Questions

QUICK TEST
1. Which four animals are skilled in spoken language?
2. Who persuades the birds that a wing is a leg?
3. Which title do the animals use to denote equality?

EXAM PRACTICE
Using at least one of the 'Key Quotations to Learn', write a paragraph explaining how the pigs change language to justify their actions in *Animal Farm*.

# Tips and Assessment Objectives

**You must be able to:** understand how to approach the exam question and meet the requirements of the mark scheme.

## Quick tips

- You will get a choice of two questions. Choose the one that best matches your knowledge, the quotations you have learned and the things you have revised.

- Make sure you know what the question is asking you. Underline key words and pay attention to the bullet point prompts that come with the question.

- You should spend about 45 minutes on your *Animal Farm* response. Allow yourself five minutes to plan your answer so there is some structure to your essay.

- Each paragraph should contain a clear idea, a relevant reference to the novel (ideally a quotation) and analysis of how Orwell conveys this idea. Whenever possible, you should link your comments to the novel's context.

- It can sometimes help, after each paragraph, to quickly re-read the question to keep yourself focussed on the exam task.

- Keep your writing concise. If you waste time 'waffling' you won't be able to include the full range of analysis and understanding that the mark scheme requires.

- It is a good idea to remember what the mark scheme is asking of you.

## AO1: Understand and respond to the novel (12 marks)

This is all about coming up with a range of points that match the question, supporting your ideas with references from the novel and writing your essay in a mature, academic style.

| Lower | Middle | Upper |
|---|---|---|
| The essay has some good ideas that are mostly relevant. Some quotations and references are used to support the ideas. | A clear essay that always focusses on the exam question. Quotations and references support ideas effectively. The response refers to different points in the novel. | A convincing, well-structured essay that answers the question fully. Quotations and references are well-chosen and integrated into sentences. The response covers the whole novel (not everything, but ideas from throughout the novel rather than just focussing on one or two sections). |

# AO2: Analyse effects of Orwell's language, form and structure (12 marks)

You need to comment on how specific words, language techniques, sentence structures and the narrative structure help Orwell to get his ideas across to readers. This could be something about a character or a larger idea that he explores through the novel. To achieve this, you will need to have learned appropriate quotations to analyse.

| Lower | Middle | Upper |
| --- | --- | --- |
| Identification of some different methods used by Orwell to convey meaning. Some subject terminology. | Explanation of Orwell's different methods. Clear understanding of the effects of these methods. Accurate use of subject terminology. | Analysis of the full range of Orwell's methods. Thorough exploration of the effects of these methods. Accurate range of subject terminology. |

# AO3: Understand the relationship between the novel and its contexts (6 marks)

For this part of the mark scheme, you need to show your understanding of how Orwell's ideas relate to the time when he was writing and the genres he wrote in.

| Lower | Middle | Upper |
| --- | --- | --- |
| Some awareness of how ideas in the novel link to its context. | References to relevant aspects of context show a clear understanding. | Exploration is linked to specific aspects of the novel's contexts to show a detailed understanding. |

# AO4: Written accuracy (4 marks)

You need to use accurate vocabulary, expression, punctuation and spelling. Although it's only four marks, this could make the difference between a lower or a higher grade.

| Lower | Middle | Upper |
| --- | --- | --- |
| Reasonable level of accuracy. Errors do not get in the way of the essay making sense. | Good level of accuracy. Vocabulary and sentence structure help to keep ideas clear. | Consistent high level of accuracy. Vocabulary and sentence structure are used to make ideas clear and precise. |

# Practice Questions

1. How does Orwell use Old Major to present ideas about freedom in *Animal Farm*?

   Write about:
   - how Orwell presents Old Major
   - how Orwell uses Old Major to explore ideas about freedom.

2. How far do you agree with the description of *Animal Farm* as a fairy tale?

   Write about:
   - how far and in what ways it is a fairy tale
   - how far and in what ways it is not a fairy tale.

3. How does Orwell present the similarities and differences between the farmers, Pilkington and Frederick, in *Animal Farm*?

   Write about:
   - the similarities and differences between Pilkington and Frederick
   - how Orwell presents these similarities and differences.

4. '*Animal Farm* shows us that revolutions always end in failure'. How far do you agree with this statement?

   Write about:
   - how Orwell writes about revolution in *Animal Farm*
   - how far and in what ways he presents the Rebellion as a failure.

5. How does Orwell present ideas about equality in *Animal Farm*?

   Write about:
   - ideas about equality presented in *Animal Farm*
   - how Orwell presents some of these ideas by the way he writes.

6. 'Snowball represents a force for good in *Animal Farm* and his expulsion signals the death of Old Major's ideals'. Explore how far you agree with this statement.

   Write about:
   - how far Orwell presents the character of Snowball as a force for good
   - how he presents Snowball's expulsion as an important turning point in the novel.

7. Explain how Orwell presents ideas about war and conflict in *Animal Farm*.

   Write about:
   - ideas about war and conflict explored in *Animal Farm*
   - how Orwell presents ideas about war and conflict.

8. How does Orwell use the character of Boxer to explore ideas about the working class in *Animal Farm*?

   Write about:
   - how Orwell presents the character of Boxer
   - how Orwell uses the character of Boxer to present ideas about the working class in the novel.

9. In *Animal Farm*, Benjamin says he will not 'meddle' and Boxer says 'Napoleon is always right'. How far and in what ways do these animals contribute to their own oppression?

   Write about:
   - how Orwell presents Benjamin and Boxer's attitudes
   - how far you think these attitudes contribute to the animals' oppression.

10. How does Orwell present the way the pigs change in *Animal Farm*?

Write about:
- how the pigs change
- how Orwell presents these changes.

11. How does Orwell use the character of Squealer to present ideas about lies and propaganda?

Write about:
- how Orwell presents Squealer in the novel
- how Orwell uses Squealer to explore ideas about lies and propaganda.

12. How does Orwell present Napoleon as a leader in *Animal Farm*?

Write about:
- how Orwell presents Napoleon in the novel
- how Orwell uses Napoleon to explore ideas about leadership.

13. 'All power corrupts. Absolute power corrupts absolutely'. How far do you think this view is supported by what happens in *Animal Farm*?

Write about:
- how power and corruption are presented in *Animal Farm*
- how far and in what ways power corrupts characters in the novel.

14. How does Orwell present female characters in *Animal Farm*?

Write about:
- what female characters Orwell writes about in *Animal Farm*
- how Orwell presents these characters by the ways he writes.

15. Explain how Orwell uses at least two of the following groups of animals in *Animal Farm*: dogs; sheep; hens; pigeons; cows.

Write about:
- how Orwell presents the animals you have chosen
- how Orwell uses these animals to explore themes and ideas.

16. 'All the other animals share responsibility for Napoleon's rise to power'. How far do you agree with this statement?

Write about:
- how far and in what ways the animals are responsible for Napoleon's rise to power
- how Orwell presents their responsibility by the way he writes.

17. Explain how Orwell uses symbols in *Animal Farm*.

Write about:
- the symbols Orwell uses in *Animal Farm*
- how Orwell uses these symbols to explore themes and ideas.

18. How important is the conflict between Napoleon and Snowball in *Animal Farm*?

Write about:
- the conflict between Napoleon and Snowball and its importance in the novel
- how Orwell presents the conflict by the way he writes.

# Planning a Character Question Response

**You must be able to:** understand what an exam question is asking you and prepare your response.

## How might an exam question on character be phrased?

A typical character question will usually look like this:

How does Orwell present Snowball as a leader in *Animal Farm*?

Write about:

- how Snowball acts as a leader
- how Orwell presents Snowball as a leader by the way he writes.

[30 marks + 4 AO4 marks]

## How do I work out what to do?

The focus of this question is clear: Snowball as a leader.

'How' is an important element of this question.

For AO1, 'how' shows that you need to display a clear understanding of what Snowball is like and how he acts, focussing on his position as a leader of the animals.

For AO2, 'how' (after the second bullet point) makes it clear that you need to analyse the different ways in which Orwell's use of language, structure and form show the reader what Snowball is like as a leader. Ideally, you should include quotations that you have learnt but, if necessary, you can make a clear reference to a specific part of the novel.

You also need to remember to link your comments to the novel's context to achieve your AO3 marks and write accurately to pick up your four AO4 marks for spelling, punctuation and grammar.

## How can I plan my essay?

You have approximately 45 minutes to write your essay.

This isn't long but you should spend the first five minutes writing a quick plan. This will help you to focus your thoughts and produce a well-structured essay.

Try to come up with five or six ideas. Each of these ideas can then be written up as a paragraph.

You can plan in whatever way you find most useful. Some students like to just make a quick list of points and then re-number them into a logical order. Spider diagrams are particularly popular; look at the example on the opposite page.

Pre-rebellion: pigs take control, Snowball one of the leading pigs
Contrast with Napoleon: more interested in revolution in other places
*... quicker in speech and more inventive, but was not considered to have the same depth of character ...*
(Context: Trotsky/Stalin)

…ailings as leader – why is he expelled?
– corruption – fails to see what Napoleon is doing – animals do not support him
*Too amazed and frightened to speak, all the animals crowded through the door to watch the chase ...*

## Snowball as a leader

Pours energy into organisation – committees – commitment to Animalism and development of ideas
*The birds did not understand Snowball's long words, but they accepted his explanation.*
(Context: Trotsky)

Plans for the windmill – shows intellect and skills – planning for the future – discussion in barn shows persuasive powers
*... in a moment Snowball's eloquence had carried them away ...*
(Context: Five-Year Plan)

Military leader at the Battle of the Cowshed: combination of tactical planning, leading from the front and personal bravery
*'No sentimentality, comrade!' cried Snowball, from whose wounds the blood was still dripping.*

## Summary

- Make sure you know what the focus of the essay is.
- Remember to analyse how Orwell conveys his ideas.
- Relate your ideas to the novel's social and historical context.

## Questions

QUICK TEST
1. What key skills do you need to show in your answer?
2. What are the benefits of quickly planning your essay?
3. Why is it better to have learned quotations for the exam?

EXAM PRACTICE
Plan a response to the following exam question:
How far does Orwell present Boxer as a heroic character in *Animal Farm*?
Write about:
- whether and how Boxer behaves in a heroic way
- how Orwell presents Boxer by the ways he writes.
[30 marks + 4 AO4 marks]

# Grade 5 Annotated Response

How does Orwell present Snowball as a leader in *Animal Farm*?

Write about:

- how Snowball acts as a leader
- how Orwell presents Snowball as a leader by the way he writes.

[30 marks + 4 AO4 marks]

*Snowball is one of the leading pigs after Old Major's death and does a lot of the preparation for the Rebellion. He is contrasted with Napoleon because he is 'quicker in speech' and clever but does not have the same 'depth of character' so maybe Napoleon is seen as a better leader (1). Snowball is more interested in getting animals on other farms to rebel than Napoleon is. This is like Trotsky and Stalin in the Russian Revolution (2).*

*He also has a lot of energy and puts a lot of effort into organising the committees after the Rebellion. He talks to them and explains what Animalism means, like when he tells the birds they have four legs. He also makes up the slogan for the ones who cannot read (3). He is taking an interest in the other animals, which means he is a good leader. The others look up to him and listen to what he says (4).*

*He shows that he is a leader in a different way when he is in charge of the Battle of the Cowshed. Orwell shows he is a very good military leader because he is clever and brave. He has studied war by reading old books he has found and he plans an ambush. In the battle, he is brave and at the front of the action. He even gets wounded. He is now a hero (5). When he tells Boxer there should be 'no sentimentality' he shows he looks at the big picture and is strong and ruthless enough to be a leader (6).*

*He shows he can be a leader in peace as well as war when he makes the plans for the windmill. This is all his idea and he is the only animal who could do anything like this. Like with the battle, he studies books and plans carefully (7). It also shows he is thinking about the future, which is something a leader should be doing. He is also doing something for the good of everyone, which Napoleon would not (8). This is also like Russia because Trotsky, who Snowball is based on, made five-year plans (9). When he tells the animals about the windmill at the meeting he uses his rhetorical skills to persuade them it is a good idea and they support him, which means they like him as a leader (10).*

*If he was a successful leader, he would not have been thrown out of the farm. There are some ways in which he is not a good leader (11). First, he does not know what Napoleon is up to when he takes away the puppies. Then the animals do not do anything to save him. They are 'too amazed and frightened'. These adjectives show how little they understand and how they do not think they should do anything. Maybe if Snowball had educated them better they would have done something and not let Napoleon take power. Like the other pigs, he thinks he is superior and is a bit corrupt. Orwell shows him as a good leader in a lot of ways but he is not successful as a leader (12).*

1. A clear statement, focussed on the question, supported by two short embedded quotations. AO1

2. A clear, if undeveloped, reference to historical context. AO3

3. A clear description of what Snowball does, referring to several points in the text; could be more clearly related to the question. Terminology used ('slogan') but the writer's methods not explored. AO1/AO2

4. Comments focussed on the question; a little generalised. AO1

5. Paragraph begins with clear focus on the question. Examples from text given but it reads a bit too much like 'story telling'. AO1

6. Brief quotation used, but not analysed, as the candidate focusses on the question. AO1

7. Focus on the question. The candidate is exploring different aspects of leadership. AO1/AO2

8. Development of idea about leadership. Reference to contrast with Napoleon implies understanding of the writer's methods. AO1/AO2

9. An inaccurate and undeveloped reference to historical context. AO1

10. Reference to methods, with appropriate terminology used. It would be better with some quotation and analysis of these 'rhetorical skills' and how the writer uses them. AO1/AO2

11. A clear point, focussed on the question. AO1

12. Point about leadership developed, using a quotation and some terminology, coming to a considered conclusion. Like the rest of the essay, this paragraph is clear and focussed but lacking in analysis. AO1/AO3

## Questions

EXAM PRACTICE

Choose a paragraph of this essay. Read it through a few times then try to rewrite and improve it. You might:

- Improve the sophistication of the language or the clarity of expression.
- Replace a reference with a quotation or use a better quotation, ensuring quotations are embedded in the sentence.
- Provide more detailed, or a wider range of, analysis.
- Use more subject terminology.
- Link some context to the analysis more effectively.

# Grade 7+ Annotated Response

A proportion of the best top-band answers will be awarded Grade 8 or Grade 9. To achieve this, you should aim for a sophisticated, fluid and nuanced response that displays flair and originality.

How does Orwell present Snowball as a leader in *Animal Farm*?

Write about:

- how Snowball acts as a leader
- how Orwell presents Snowball as a leader by the way he writes.      [30 marks + 4 AO4 marks]

*After Old Major's death, Snowball is named by Orwell as one of the leading pigs who develop Old Major's teachings 'into a complete system of thought'. Snowball is a leader but he is not <u>the</u> leader (1). He is defined in relation to Napoleon. He is 'quicker in speech and more inventive', the comparative adjectives here being given as fact. However, he is 'not considered to have the same depth of character'. The verb 'considered' signals that Napoleon's 'depth of character' is an opinion. The writer chooses not to explore what this 'depth' might mean, implying that it means very little. Yet, in the end, the less clever, less inventive pig will be <u>the</u> leader (2).*

*Snowball is indefatigable in organising committees and explaining the ideas of Animalism. In this he resembles Leon Trotsky, the Russian leader whose fate he will also share (3). He leads by getting involved with others and adapting his message to their needs, as when he reduces the Commandments to the slogan 'Four legs good, two legs bad' for those who cannot read. He demonstrates his persuasive and rhetorical powers when he convinces the birds that they have four legs. They accept his explanation, as Mollie accepts that sugar and ribbons are 'badges of slavery'. We are, however, left with the feeling that these animals are not totally convinced (4).*

*Snowball's leadership qualities come to the fore when he takes on the role of military leader before and during the Battle of the Cowshed, recalling Trotsky's role after the Russian Revolution. At this point in the story, Snowball could be described as the protagonist as he drives the action, while Napoleon lurks in the background (5). Orwell presents him as a very good military leader. Not only is he a strategist, effectively using the lessons he has learned from his study of Julius Caesar, but he is shown in the thick of the battle. When he says there should be 'no sentimentality' and that 'war is war', he shows the strength of character and single-mindedness that has enabled him to lead. These sentiments gain power from the fact that he is still bleeding from his wounds (6).*

*However, he is still not the only leader and, unlike his antagonist Napoleon, he does not do anything to make himself powerful. Nevertheless, he shows the qualities of a peacetime leader when he makes the plans for the windmill (the equivalent of Stalin's 'five-year plans' for the USSR, which many think were based on Trotsky's ideas), showing that he thinks about the future of the farm. Furthermore, he puts his 'eloquence' to good use at the meeting, persuading the other animals of the merits of his scheme.*

*So why does this meeting, a crucial turning point in the plot, lead to Napoleon becoming the undisputed leader (7)?*

*The narrator chooses not to explore the pigs' thoughts so we are not told whether Snowball sees himself as a leader. Some readers may feel that he really believes that 'all animals are equal' and only takes on responsibility because his superior talent makes it 'natural' for him to do so. Others might interpret his disagreements with Napoleon as showing that they are competing for leadership (8). If this is so, Snowball makes mistakes which lead to his failure. He does not know what Napoleon is up to when he takes away the puppies. Also, the fact that the animals are 'too amazed and frightened' to help him suggests that, despite his efforts to spread the message, they do not understand that Animalism is under threat and, crucially, do not see him as their leader (9).*

*Orwell presents Snowball as having many of the qualities that might make a good leader but, ultimately, he is unsuccessful. As Napoleon leads the farm into totalitarianism, Snowball acquires the aura of the 'lost leader', just as Trotsky did, leaving readers wondering whether things would have turned out differently had he rather than Napoleon become <u>the</u> leader (10).*

1.  A clear statement, addressing the question, well supported by an embedded quotation. AO1

2.  Well-developed analysis of the writer's use of language, focussed on the question, using accurate terminology. AO2

3.  A clear and relevant reference to historical context. AO3

4.  Develops the discussion about leadership, considering what it means and using quotations and terminology well. AO1/AO2

5.  Maintains close focus on the question, considering another idea about leadership through consideration of the writer's use of form and structure. Uses appropriate terminology. Well integrated reference to context. AO1/AO2/AO3

6.  Clearly explains the assertion made at the start of the paragraph, using quotations to support thoughtful points. AO1

7.  More thoughtful argument, maintaining focus and referring skilfully to historical context. AO1/AO3

8.  Consideration of Orwell's methods leads to an acknowledgment of possible alternative interpretations. AO1/AO2/AO3

9.  Continued thoughtful consideration of the question, supported by relevant references to the text. AO1

10. Concluding paragraph brings together ideas about Snowball as a leader, referring to the context and bringing us back to the opening of the essay. The candidate has used language accurately and in a sophisticated way. AO1/AO3/AO4

## Questions

EXAM PRACTICE

Spend 45 minutes writing an answer to the following question:

How far does Orwell present Boxer as a heroic character in *Animal Farm*?

Write about:

*   whether and how Boxer behaves in a heroic way
*   how Orwell presents Boxer by the way he writes.     [30 marks + 4 AO4 marks]

Remember to use the plan you have already prepared.

# Planning a Theme Question Response

**You must be able to:** understand what an exam question is asking you and prepare your response.

## How might an exam question on character be phrased?

A typical theme question will read like this:

How does Orwell present ideas about freedom in *Animal Farm*?

Write about:

- what ideas about freedom are presented in *Animal Farm*
- how Orwell presents some of these ideas by the way he writes.

[30 marks + 4 AO4 marks]

## How do I work out what to do?

The focus of this question is clear: ideas about freedom.

'What' and 'how' are important elements of this question.

For AO1, 'what' shows that you need to display a clear understanding of the different ideas about what freedom means expressed in the novel.

For AO2, 'how' makes it clear that you need to analyse the different ways in which Orwell's use of language, structure and form help to show these ideas. Ideally, you should include quotations that you have learnt but, if necessary, you can make a clear reference to a specific part of the novel.

You also need to remember to link your comments to the novel's context to achieve your AO3 marks and write accurately to pick up your four AO4 marks for spelling, punctuation and grammar.

## How can I plan my essay?

You have approximately 45 minutes to write your essay.

This isn't long but you should spend the first five minutes writing a quick plan. This will help you to focus your thoughts and produce a well-structured essay.

Try to come up with five or six ideas. Each of these ideas can then be written up as a paragraph.

You can plan in whatever way you find most useful. Some students like to just make a quick list of points and then re-number them into a logical order. Spider diagrams are particularly popular; look at the example on the opposite page.

## Ideas about freedom

Old Major's explanation of how they are not free and idealistic idea of what freedom is like – dream – song
*Almost overnight we could become rich and free ...*
(Context: ideals of Russian Revolution – Lenin)

uman farmers see animals working like slaves
*They worked diligently, hardly raising their heads from the ground ...*

What freedom means after the Rebellion – destruction of symbols of oppression – linked to democracy, equality and cooperation
*... the bits, the nose-rings, the dog-chains, the cruel knives ...*
*The animals were happy as they had never conceived it possible to be.*

Vhat does liberty mean? lover clings on to idea of •erty making things better but it has not brought the promised benefits
*All that year the animals worked like slaves.*
*.. in those days they had •een slaves and now they •re free, and that made all the difference ...*
(Context: reality of life in USSR and other post-revolution states)

Erosion of liberty after Snowball's expulsion – no meetings – 'orders' from Napoleon – extra hours and low rations imposed
*But sometimes you might make the wrong decisions, comrades, and then where would we be?*
(Context: freedom of speech)

Examples of how liberty has limits – Mollie – the cat – horses still harnessing themselves to ploughs – the Commandments
*... those ribbons that you are devoted to are the badge of slavery.*
(Snowball: Chapter 2)

## Summary

- Make sure you know what the focus of the essay is.
- Remember to analyse how ideas are conveyed by Orwell.
- Try to relate your ideas to the novel's social and historical context.

## Questions

QUICK TEST
1. What key skills do you need to show in your answer?
2. What are the benefits of quickly planning your essay?
3. Why is it better to have learned quotations for the exam?

EXAM PRACTICE
Plan a response to the following exam question:
How does Orwell present ideas about revolution in *Animal Farm*? Write about:
- what ideas about revolution are presented
- how Orwell presents these ideas by the way he writes.
[30 marks + 4 AO4 marks]

How does Orwell present ideas about freedom in *Animal Farm*?

Write about:

- what ideas about freedom are presented in *Animal Farm*
- how Orwell presents some of these ideas by the way he writes.

[30 marks + 4 AO4 marks]

In Chapter 1, Old Major talks to the animals about his dream of freedom from human beings. 'Overnight we could become rich and free' (1). He blames human beings for everything that is wrong and says that without humans their lives will be much better. He tells them about his dream of how their lives will be once they are free. He does not explain how it will come about except that they must get rid of man so they will be free (2). He is like Lenin in the Russian Revolution (3).

When they do rebel, the animals show that they are free by running around the farm and enjoying everything they see, although Orwell focusses on the way they own the farm rather than being free, it is 'theirs' (4). He shows what he means by freedom when he describes the animals destroying symbols of slavery, such as harnesses and knives. Now there are no humans, they are not controlled or treated badly (5).

The problem is that someone still has to manage the farm and, because they are 'clever', it is the pigs who do this. They supervise the others. Also, the horses 'harness themselves' to the machines so they can work. This does not sound like being free but Orwell says 'no bits or reins', cruel things people use are used, so at least they are more free than they were. In general, the animals do things willingly (6). However, there is an example of an animal not getting to do what they want when Snowball tells Mollie that her ribbons show she is a slave. She does not feel free so she escapes from the farm and returns to what the others see as slavery, pulling a cart. Another idea of freedom is given by the cat. She just does whatever she wants but she always has done (7).

Up to when Snowball goes, the animals have a lot more freedom but when Napoleon takes over things start to go back to how they were when Jones was in charge. First of all, he says there will be no more meetings because they might make the wrong decisions. Now they have no freedom of speech, which is an important thing that governments often try to stop (8). Napoleon gives 'orders' for everything that has to be done. The word 'orders' is used a lot and shows that others have to obey so they are not really free (9).

After the executions, the animals are described as working 'like slaves', which shows that their freedom has gone. However, they do not seem to realise that it has. Clover thinks what they have now is not what they fought for but she still thinks it is better because 'then they were slaves'. The reader would think they are slaves now so their freedom does not mean much. This reflects life in Russia after the revolution when people did not have much freedom (10).

*At the end when the farmers come to inspect Animal Farm, the animals are described as working with their heads down and not knowing whether to be more frightened of the humans or the animals. This is like a description of slavery, not freedom. They were free for a time but now they are not (11).*

1. The opening sentence focusses on the question in a clear, if simple, way and there is a relevant quotation, although it would be better if it were embedded. AO1

2. Reference to the text, paraphrasing what Old Major says, with some interpretation ('idealised'). AO1

3. A brief contextual reference, relevant but undeveloped. AO3

4. An interesting point, supported by quotation, but undeveloped. The written expression is fairly clear but lacks accuracy and sophistication. AO1/AO4

5. Focus on the question, with some discussion of Orwell's methods, using correct terminology ('symbols'). AO1/AO2

6. A good attempt to explore further 'ideas about freedom'. Brief reference to use of language. AO1/AO2

7. Moves on to another, relevant point about ideas of freedom, using quotation effectively. The point about the cat is not properly explained. AO1

8. Focusses on the question with a new point about freedom, related to historical and social context. Awareness of structure shown. AO1/AO2/AO3

9. Consideration of use of language linked to question. AO2

10. Clear explanation, exploring ideas of freedom, supported by relevant quotation. Point linked to historical context. AO1/AO3

11. Final paragraph shows understanding of the text and the question, making a clear point with an implied understanding of context. AO1/AO3

## Questions

EXAM PRACTICE

Choose a paragraph of this essay. Read it through a few times then try to rewrite and improve it. You might:

- Improve the sophistication of the language and the clarity of expression.
- Replace a reference with a quotation or use a better quotation, ensuring quotations are embedded in the sentence.
- Provide more detailed, or a wider range of, analysis.
- Use more subject terminology.
- Link some context to the analysis more effectively.

# Grade 7+ Annotated Response

A proportion of the best top-band answers will be awarded Grade 8 or Grade 9. To achieve this, you should aim for a sophisticated, fluid and nuanced response that displays flair and originality.

How does Orwell present ideas about freedom in *Animal Farm*?

Write about:

- what ideas about freedom are presented in *Animal Farm*
- how Orwell presents some of these ideas by the way he writes.    [30 marks + 4 AO4 marks]

*Old Major's speech to the animals focusses on the idea of freedom, which he defines in terms of their relationship to human beings: if they rebel they 'will be rich and free' (1). He claims the song 'Beasts of England' came to him in a 'dream', playing on different connotations of that word: it is both inspiration and an aspiration. The song's images of a 'golden future' full of 'riches' create a pastoral idyll. The simplicity of its message is reflected in its simple regular form and strong rhythm (2). Old Major is an idealist and, unlike Lenin, who played a similar role before the Russian Revolution, does not live to see the consequences of revolt. He inspires his followers to fight for freedom but he does not define what freedom means (3).*

*After the Rebellion, the animals are depicted enjoying a landscape that is 'sweet' and 'rich' like the England of the song and Orwell stresses that 'everything that they could see was theirs'. The implication is that freedom necessitates control, which comes from ownership, an idea that reflects socialist thinking (4). The animals celebrate their freedom by destroying symbols of Man's control, such as harnesses, knives and whips. The power of these symbols comes from the physical pain they inflict, so it is interesting that Snowball extends the definition of symbols of slavery to ribbons and even Boxer's hat (5).*

*This introduces the issue of how slavery and freedom should be defined. Snowball fails to convince Mollie that her ribbons are a 'badge of slavery'. Her escape from the farm suggests that she does not feel free. Moses has also chosen to leave the farm and the cat does as she pleases. Orwell uses these three animals to raise questions about individual freedom. For the pigs, pulling a cart represents slavery but Mollie chooses to do it, so can she be said to be enslaved (6)? Orwell presents an example of how freedom cannot be absolute when he describes how the pigs 'assume leadership'. He uses free indirect discourse to seamlessly move from reporting that they 'did not actually work' to giving their justification for this: 'With their superior knowledge it was natural' (7). This may be ironic but it still raises the question of how things can be managed – on a farm or in a country – if everyone is free. Not only do the pigs supervise the others but the horses 'harness themselves' to the machines. This does not sound like being free but 'no bits or reins' are needed, suggesting some limits on freedom are acceptable if they are necessary and adopted willingly (8).*

*Despite limits on freedom, the animals have control and gain benefits from their liberty. However, the expulsion of Snowball and Napoleon's taking of power signal a turning point in the novel. Napoleon banishes meetings because the others 'might not make the right decisions', thereby abolishing free speech and democratic decision making. This reflects the erosion of freedom that so often occurs in post-*

*revolutionary societies, including the USSR. Now Napoleon gives 'orders' for everything that has to be done. The word 'orders' is used frequently from now on, as is the title 'Leader'. With Napoleon using dogs to instil fear and carrying a whip, the most hated symbol of Man's tyranny, the animals must obey him and so are no longer free (9).*

*After the purge, the animals are described as working 'like slaves'. Yet they cling to the idea that they are still free. They accept hardships because 'they had been slaves and now they were free'. It may be that the animals are being fooled by the pigs into believing something that is not true. On the other hand, Orwell might be suggesting that freedom is an* **abstract** *concept and that feeling free is not always about facts. They may work 'like slaves' but they are not slaves and that, in Squealer's words, makes 'all the difference' (10).*

*However, just how little difference it makes is shown in the final chapter when the human farmers come to inspect Animal Farm. The animals work with their heads down 'not knowing whether to be more frightened of the pigs or of the human visitors'. This is an image of slavery, not freedom. Orwell has presented freedom as an ideal to aspire to but he also demonstrates how fragile a concept it is and how easily it can be destroyed (11).*

1. A clear point, focussed on the question and supported by a relevant quotation. AO1

2. Detailed analysis of the writer's use of language and form. AO2

3. Relevant point made about ideas of freedom, linked to historical context. AO1/AO3

4. Explores a new idea about freedom, rooted in context. AO1/AO3

5. Thoughtful exploration of ideas, referring to writer's methods and using appropriate terminology. AO1/AO2

6. Continues exploring the question, making new points, supported by examples from the text. AO1

7. Sophisticated terminology used to support analysis of the writer's methods. AO2

8. Another quite sophisticated point made, convincingly expressed. An understanding of context is an important part of the points now being made. AO1/AO3/AO4

9. This paragraph raises more issues about freedom, using quotations effectively and showing understanding of the writer's methods as well as of the historical and social contexts. AO1/AO2/AO3

10. Thoughtful exploration of alternative interpretations, maintaining focus on the question to the end. AO1/AO3

11. Effective concluding paragraph, summarising the candidate's response to the question. AO1/AO3/AO4

> ## Questions
>
> EXAM PRACTICE
> Spend 45 minutes writing an answer to the following question:
> How does Orwell present ideas about revolution in *Animal Farm*? Write about:
> • what ideas about revolution are presented
> • how Orwell presents these ideas by the way he writes.
> [30 marks + 4 AO4 marks]
> Remember to use the plan you have already prepared.

# Glossary

**Abstract concept (adj.)** – not concrete or practical but theoretical.

**Active verb** – a verb in the active voice, when the subject is the thing or person acting, for example, 'the dog bit the boy'.

**Adjective** – a word that describes a noun.

**Allegory (adj. allegorical)** – see page 22.

**Anecdote** – a brief story, used to illustrate a point.

**Antagonist** – the person in a story who opposes the protagonist.

**Anthem** – a song of praise, often for a nation (national anthem).

**Anthropomorphism (adj. anthropomorphic)** – writing about animals as if they were human.

**Antipathy** – strong, lasting dislike.

**Aristocracy** – the ruling class, whose power is based on their inherited wealth.

**Atmosphere** – a tone, mood or general feeling.

**Attitude** – feeling about or opinion of something or someone.

**Authoritarian** – believing in strict obedience to authority.

**Bureaucracy** – government officials; excessive administration or management.

**Capitalism** – economic and political system based on private ownership of property and industry.

**Chronological** – ordered according to time.

**Climax** – the high or most dramatic point of a story, usually near the end.

**Communism** – social and political system based on public ownership. See page 20.

**Complicit** – being a partner in wrongdoing.

**Connotation** – an implied meaning or something suggested by association.

**Crisis** – a decisive moment.

**Despotism** – rule by a despot (someone who is an absolute ruler/tyrant).

**Diction** – choice of vocabulary.

**Eloquence (adj. eloquent)** – speaking fluently and well.

**Emotive** – creating or describing strong emotions.

**Euphemism** – the use of mild or vague expressions instead of harsh or blunt ones, for example, saying 'passed away' instead of 'died'.

**Exposition** – the opening part of a novel or play where setting and characters are introduced.

**Fable** – a story with a moral, often featuring animals behaving like humans, See page 22.

**Fascism** – extreme right-wing nationalist movement. See page 20.

**Free indirect discourse (or free indirect style)** – a way of presenting the thoughts and feelings of a character from that character's point of view by combining features of direct and indirect discourse. For example, if direct discourse (like direct speech) were: '*I will propose tomorrow*', *he thought* indirect discourse would be: *He thought that he would propose on the following day.* Free indirect discourse might be: *He would propose tomorrow.*

**Gullible** – easily taken in or fooled.

**Hypocrisy** – insincerity, especially saying one thing and doing another.

**Ideal (noun)** – an idea of perfection.

**Idealistic** – believing in ideals.

**Incongruity (adj. incongruous)** – not fitting/ being out of place.

**Image/Imagery** – words used to create a picture in the imagination.

**Imperative** – an order or command.

**Imply** – to suggest something that is not expressly stated.

**Inciting incident** – an event that starts off a story.

**The Industrial Revolution** – the period of history (eighteenth to nineteenth centuries) when the use of machinery increased, leading to big factories and causing people to leave the countryside for work in towns and cities.

**Infer (noun inference)** – to deduce something that is not openly stated.

**Irony (adj. ironic)** – when words are used to imply an opposite meaning.

**Juxtaposition** – the placing of two things (especially words) next to each other. Note that the use of this word does **not** necessarily imply contrast.

Knacker – someone who buys old horses for slaughter.

Knoll – a small hill or mound.

Materialism – greater interest in material things than in spiritual matters.

Means of production – ways in which food and goods are made, for example, farms and factories.

Minor sentence – a 'sentence' that does not contain a verb but starts with a capital letter and ends with a full stop.

Mutiny – a rebellion against authority (usually in the armed forces).

Nationalisation (vb. nationalise) – taking things such as companies into state ownership.

Noun – a naming word.

Oppression – tyrannical or harsh government. See page 44.

Oppressor – someone who oppresses others.

Orator – a skilful public speaker.

Orchard – a piece of land with fruit trees.

Overtly – openly or directly.

Oxymoron (adj. oxymoronic) – two contradictory words placed together, for example, 'bitter sweet'.

Paddock – a small field, especially for keeping horses in.

Pastoral idyll – a romanticised idea of rural life.

Pasture – land for grazing.

Personification (vb. personify) – writing about an idea or object as if it were human.

Politburo – the ruling body of the Communist Party in the USSR.

Present participle – the part of the verb used to convey ongoing action, ending in 'ing'.

Proletariat (adj. proletarian) – the people/the working classes.

Propaganda – information, especially of a biased or misleading nature, used to promote a political cause or point of view.

Protagonist – the main character.

Purge – the act of making clean. Politically, getting rid of those thought undesirable.

Rhetoric – the art of speaking.

Rhetorical device – a technique used in speaking.

Rhetorical question – a question that that the speaker does not expect to be answered.

Rural – of the countryside.

Russian Orthodox Church – a denomination of Christianity, the official church of Russia.

Satire (adj. satirical) – literature that uses humour to criticise people or society. See pages 22–23.

Scapegoat – someone who is blamed for what others have done.

Secular – not concerned with religion.

Slogan – a catchy phrase.

Simple sentence – a sentence containing only one clause, including a subject and a verb.

Socialism – political and economic theory advocating state control of production.

Socialist – someone who believes in socialism.

Social reform – changing society, usually with the intention of improving it.

Spanish Civil War – A war fought in Spain between 1936 and 1939. The Republicans, who supported the elected government but included many revolutionary groups, were defeated by the Nationalists, a fascist party led by General Franco. Franco ruled Spain until 1975.

Sycophant (adj. sycophantic) – a flatterer.

Symbol (adj. symbolic) – an object use to represent an idea.

Symbolise – (of an object) to represent a specific idea or meaning.

Totalitarianism (adj. totalitarian) – one-party government requiring total subservience to the state. See page 20.

Turning point – a point in a story when things change significantly.

Tyranny (adj. tyrannical, adv. tyrannically) – cruel use of authority.

Union of Soviet Socialist Republics (USSR) – (1922–1991) the name given to the former Russian Empire, consisting of Russia and other states, after the Russian Revolution (1917). A 'soviet' was a workers' committee.

Verb – a doing, feeling, thinking or being word.

# Answers

**Pages 4–5**

Quick Test

1. They are summoned by Old Major, who has had a dream.
2. Man.
3. Napoleon, Snowball and Squealer.
4. The Seven Commandments.

Exam Practice

Answers might include the following: the sense of anticipation built by the animals' preparations; the mundane, almost accidental events that cause the Rebellion; the unity of the animals; the very quick way in which it happens; the animals' feelings afterwards.

Analysis might include the use of violent **diction** ('kicked', 'thrashing', etc.), the switch from the animals' to the humans' point of view and the creation of sympathy for the animals through the contrast between their hard work and commitment and the farmer's laziness.

**Pages 6–7**

Quick Test

1. They have meetings in the barn.
2. Napoleon and Snowball.
3. They send out the pigeons.
4. Julius Caesar.

Exam Practice

Answers might focus on the sense of cooperation and progress, how the animals put their principles into practice and their success at The Battle of the Cowshed. They might also consider how the seeds are sown for later changes/problems, such as the disappearance of the milk.

Analysis might include the way in which the contribution of each animal or group of animals is described, the absurd comedy of animals doing human tasks and how the writer makes us believe in it, as well as the reactions of the animals to their achievements.

**Pages 8–9**

Quick Test

1. To generate electricity.
2. The green flag and Old Major's skull.
3. Sleeping in beds.

Exam Practice

Answers might explore the increasing tension between Napoleon and Snowball, the expulsion of Snowball, the animals' reaction to this, the increasing unease among the animals, and Napoleon's gradual acquisition of more power. Analysis might include how Orwell raises the tension in Chapter 5, describing the increasing conflict in the barn apparently building to Snowball's victory, the appearance of the dogs, the mystery of their origin, the excitement of the chase conveyed by the **present participles** used to describe the dogs ('baying', 'growling') and the simple past verbs conveying action ('dashed', 'slipped', 'whisked').

**Pages 10–11**

Quick Test

1. Mr Pilkington and Mr Frederick.
2. Snowball.
3. He gives Napoleon forged banknotes.

Exam Practice

Answers could focus on the hens' rebellion and the executions in Chapter 7 or The Battle of the Windmill in Chapter 8. Analysis might focus on the way the crushing of the hens' revolt is used to prepare the reader for the executions, the vocabulary used to convey Napoleon's authority ('ordered', 'surveyed' and the sense of fear and anticipation, 'They all cowered silently'), the focus on noises such as squealing and shrieking and the contrast between the frenzy of the dogs' attack and the calm with which the executions are performed.

**Pages 12–13**

Quick Test

1. The pigs.
2. Four legs good, two legs better.
3. The farm's name is to be changed back to Manor Farm; there will be no flag; there will be no marching past Old Major's skull.

Exam Practice

Answers might focus on the comic, satirical tone of Orwell's description of the pigs walking on hind legs and dressing as humans and how this becomes chilling as they 'become' humans at the end. Analysis might include the absurdity of the pigs who are 'a little unsteady', the impact of the isolated simple sentence, 'He carried a whip in his trotter', the **incongruity** of domestic details such as the wireless, the magazines and the clothes, and the way the scene in the farmhouse is seen via Clover's 'dim old eyes'.

**Pages 14–15**

Quick Test

1. Chronological order.
2. The Battle of the Cowshed; the expulsion of Snowball; the Battle of the Windmill.
3. How the pigs have changed and betrayed the principles of Animalism.
4. The pigs become indistinguishable from humans.

Exam Practice

Answers might include the apparent normality of the opening sentences before focus shifts to the animals, the exposition in Chapter 1 introducing the characters and ideas, the way each chapter builds to a climax and ends with an incident that shows how things are changing, the use of chronological order and how the events described parallel the history of Russia, the reflective mood of the beginning of Chapter 10 and how it is changed by the shocking revelation at the end.

**Pages 16–17**
Quick Test
1. The Spanish Civil War.
2. The USSR.
3. The Labour Party.

Exam Practice
Answers might include the following: the mutual distrust between Pilkington and Frederick; their lack of concern for Jones but fear for their own future, reflecting reactions to the Russian Revolution; the description of their contrasting farms, related to Germany and the rest of Europe; Napoleon's dealings with them, reflecting Stalin's dealings with capitalist countries; Frederick as Hitler, shown in his cruelty; his double-crossing of Napoleon and invasion of the farm, reflecting the German invasion of the USSR; the dinner in the farmhouse reflecting Lenin's alliance with the Western powers in the Second World War.

**Pages 18–19**
Quick Test
1. They decide to move into it.
2. In the farmyard.
3. The windmill.

Exam Practice
Answers might include the following: the way Orwell describes a pastoral idyll when the animals enjoy their surroundings; how the contents of the farmhouse **symbolise** privilege but are later adopted by the pigs; symbolism of the barn and how changes there reflect the betrayal of principles; the symbolism of the windmill and descriptions of its destruction.

**Pages 20–21**
Quick Test
1. No.
2. Communism.
3. Italy, Spain, Germany.

Exam Practice
Answers might include the sense of occasion created for the meeting in the barn, the respect others have for Old Major, the parallels between the animals' situation and that of the workers in Russia, the similarities between his ideas and Lenin's communism and his use of persuasive rhetorical devices such as anecdote, rhetorical questions and emotive language.

**Pages 22–23**
Quick Test
1. A Fairy Story.
2. Animals.
3. By ridiculing (making fun of) them.

Exam Practice
Answers might include the use of animals to convey ideas about humans, the absurdity of the animals' behaviour used to satirise the USSR, parallels between the meeting with the farmers and historical events, differences between the novel's ending and a fairy tale ending, moral and political lessons to be learned from the story and the simplicity of the form used to convey a serious message (chronological order, relatively simple language).

**Pages 24–25**
Quick Test
1. V.I. Lenin.
2. The NKVD (secret police).
3. He deceives Napoleon and invades the farm as Germany invaded the USSR during the Second World War.

Exam Practice
Answers might include the cooperation and positive spirit among the animals, the decision-making process, better conditions and a sense of equality, better education, Snowball's plans reflecting the Five-Year Plans, the use of propaganda, the corruption of the leaders, how Napoleon's rise reflects the rise of Stalin, Napoleon's execution and Stalin's purges, lies told to the animals and shortages and near starvation

**Pages 26–27**
Quick Test
1. A boar.
2. V.I. Lenin.
3. He disinters his skull and displays it under the flag.

Exam Practice
Answers might include the description of his appearance and how the animals regard him, the listing of all the animals in his audience, which shows his importance, his constant use of the term 'comrades', his use of direct address and examples to include his listeners, the way he invokes a 'dream' to inspire his listeners, his skilled used of rhetorical devices and his use of the song.

**Pages 28–29**
Quick Test
1. Joseph Stalin.
2. Snowball.
3. His vanity, arrogance and love of power.

Exam Practice
Answers might focus on Napoleon's increasing isolation, his control of the dogs, his use of Squealer to put out propaganda and lies, his acquisition of titles and decorations, and his treatment of dissent.

Analysis might include the contrast between the titles 'comrade' and 'leader' and how they are now **juxtaposed**, the combination of showy power and real tyranny shown by his use of the cockerel and the dogs, the satire of Stalin shown in the list of absurd titles such as 'Ducklings' Friend' and Minimus's song, and the **symbolism** of inscribing the song on the barn wall opposite the Commandments.

**Pages 30–31**
Quick Test
1. Leon Trotsky.
2. He uses military tactics to ambush the humans.
3. Four pigs ('young porkers').

Exam Practice
Answers might focus on his role as antagonist to Napoleon, his similarity to Trotsky, the active role he takes after the Rebellion, his plans for the windmill, his leadership at the Battle of the Cowshed or his expulsion by Napoleon and Napoleon's re-invention of him

Analysis might focus on the following: diction used to convey his energy ('vivacious', 'quicker') and his active part in the

# Answers

battle ('dashed', 'flung'); similar diction used during his escape; the contrast between his involvement with the other animals and Napoleon's focus on the dogs; contrast between his eloquence and Napoleon's brevity and quiet speech; his portrayal as both an intellectual and military leader.

### Pages 32–33
Quick Test
1. He skips from side to side.
2. He holds the ladder.
3. When Boxer collapses.

Exam Practice

Answers could focus on his explanation of why Napoleon changes how things are done, his lies about Snowball, his re-telling of the Battle of the Windmill, his justification of Napoleon dealing with Frederick or his lies about Boxer's death.

Analysis might include the following: the meaning of his 'skipping'; contrast between his 'twinkling' eyes and how he skips 'merrily' and his 'sly' and 'ugly' looks; use of rhetorical questions; constant use of Napoleon's name; use of the threat of Jones's return; the physical presence of the dogs backing him up.

### Pages 34–35
Quick Test
1. 'I must work harder'
2. Napoleon.
3. The knacker's.

Exam Practice

Answers might focus on his loyalty, hard work, stupidity, trust in Napoleon, reputation with the other animals and treatment by Napoleon.

Analysis might include his two slogans and how slogans can both strengthen and weaken those who adopt them, the frequent references to his physical strength and capacity for hard work, the contrast of his usual gentleness with his 'terrifying' appearance in the battle, the ease with which he is controlled and the affection shown to him by Clover and Benjamin.

### Pages 36–37
Quick Test
1. Boxer.
2. Sugar and ribbons.
3. Clover.

Exam Practice

Answers might focus on her concern about breaches of the Commandments, her thoughts after the executions and her inability to express them, her acceptance of the changes despite her doubts and her part in seeing the pigs change. Analysis might include the repetition of her action in going to the barn with Muriel, Orwell's use of free indirect discourse in conveying her thoughts, contrast between her nostalgia for the time when she protected the ducklings and the present atmosphere of fear and distrust, the repetition of 'it was not for this' and the significance of her singing of 'Beasts of England' followed by Napoleon's ban on the song.

### Pages 38–39
Quick Test
1. He believes that there is nothing worth reading.
2. The blowing up of the windmill.
3. Because they have not realised where the van is taking Boxer.

Exam Practice

Answers might focus on his intelligence, his cynicism, his refusal to get involved in things and his affection for Boxer. Analysis might include his 'cryptic' remarks to other animals, the significance of his not wanting to 'meddle', the description of how he works after the Rebellion, the language he uses to address the other animals ('Fools!'), the description of his action when Boxer is taken away and to what extent he is complicit in the pigs' rise to power.

### Pages 40–41
Quick Test
1. A pig who writes poems.
2. Napoleon takes them away and trains them to be his bodyguards/secret police.
3. She kicks in the door to the food store.

Exam Practice

Dogs: Answers might focus on the difference between the older dogs and the dogs trained by Napoleon, the use of dogs to control and frighten the other animals and the savagery they display. Analysis might include consideration of how Orwell uses characteristics associated with dogs such as loyalty, hunting instincts and the ability to control other animals (e.g. sheep), the violent language used to describe them and parallels with Stalin's NKVD.

Hens: Answers should focus on their rebellion, including its causes and effects. Analysis might include their characterisation as not being intelligent, how they accuse the pigs of being 'murderers' but then destroy their own eggs, the mystery/secrecy surrounding how the rebellion is put down and its structural use in building up to the purges.

### Pages 42–43
Quick Test
1. Neglect the farm.
2. Foxwood and Pinchfield.
3. Solicitor.

Exam Practice

Answers could focus on Jones, Fredrick, Whymper or Pilkington, or discuss the way humans are portrayed in general. They might mention how humans are seen as 'the enemy', parallels between them and historical figures (e.g. the Tsar and Hitler), the significance of Napoleon starting to deal with them despite the principles of Animalism, their depiction as oppressors and aggressors, their reactions to Animal Farm and the way the pigs' increasing resemblance to them shows the extent of their corruption.

**Page 44–45**

Quick Test

1. Any three from: chains, knives, reins, harnesses, whips.
2. Whips.
3. By refusing to meddle.

Exam Practice

Answers might include the pigs' early assumption of leadership based on their 'superior intelligence', their domination of meetings, the expulsion of Snowball as a turning point and Napoleon's acquisition of greater power, lack of opposition to them, Napoleon's use of fear to control, the symbols of power and how their increasing power is reflected in their growing resemblance to humans.

**Pages 46–47**

Quick Test

1. Through rebellion.
2. The Seventh Commandment.
3. Mollie.

Exam Practice

Analysis might focus on Old Major's introduction of the idea, his reference to inequalities in strength and intelligence, the importance of the Seventh Commandment, the pigs' leadership apparently contradicting the idea of equality, the pigs' gradual acquisition of power and privilege, division between pigs and others shown by the pigs living in the house, language used about Napoleon ('our Leader', 'orders'), the continuation of a pretence of equality through the use of 'comrade' and the change to the Commandments.

**Pages 48–49**

Quick Test

1. Greed and power.
2. By keeping the milk and apples for themselves.
3. Mollie and Moses.

Exam Practice

Answers could focus on the turning point of the keeping of the apples, the relationship between the pigs' materialism and their increasing power, the drinking of alcohol, the attraction of money and dealings with humans, corruption of the ideas of Animalism, corruption of the pigs, corruption of Mollie and Moses, how far power corrupts and how far greed corrupts.

**Pages 50–51**

Quick Test

1. Chasing rats.
2. Violence does not come naturally to him.
3. Courageous and unified.

Exam Practice

Answers might focus on the creation of sympathy for the animals and **antipathy** to the humans, rising and falling tension as the battles ebb and flow, the use of **active verbs** to create excitement, the use of animal characteristics (especially to create comedy in the Battle of the Cowshed), the violent diction of the Battle of the Windmill, the focus on injuries and deaths, the differences between human and animal violence and the justified use of violence in a good cause.

**Pages 52–53**

Quick Test

1. He stands in front of the milk buckets.
2. Snowball.
3. During the Battle of the Cowshed.

Exam Practice

Answers might focus on the way the pigs' lies get bigger throughout the novel, how easily the other animals are deceived, the changes to the Commandments, Napoleon's use of Squealer to deceive the animals, the way he boasts of the deception of Whymper and Snowball's use of deceit in the battle. Analysis might include Napoleon and Squealer's use of rhetorical questions, Napoleon's quiet manner, the way Squealer is described when he is lying ('skipping') and his use of detail and emotive language.

**Pages 54–55**

Quick Test

1. Sugarcandy Mountain.
2. By saying that they do not believe Moses but giving him an allowance of beer.
3. Hoisting the flag and singing 'Beasts of England'.

Exam Practice

Answers might focus on the use of Moses to represent religion or the animals' adoption of religious-style ritual. Analysis might focus on Moses' physical appearance, parallels to the Russian Orthodox Church, his relationship to the humans, details of Sugarcandy Mountain and its similarity to Old Major's dream, the simple reference to the pigs' attitude when he returns, the similarity of the Commandments to the Ten Commandments, the pigs' use of ritual and similarities between the animals' ceremonies and religious ceremonies.

**Pages 56–57**

Quick Test

1. Old Major, Snowball, Squealer and Moses.
2. Snowball.
3. Comrade.

Exam Practice

Answers might focus on Snowball and Squealer's skill with language and how it is used to change meaning, how language skills give power or the pigs' use of revolutionary language to disguise what they are doing. Analysis might include the use of logic to arrive at absurd conclusions, rhetorical devices used to persuade, juxtaposition of the words 'comrade' and 'leader', the pigs' constant use of 'comrade' to denote equality, the use of euphemisms such as 'readjustment' instead of 'reduction' and the use of words to mean the opposite of their true meaning.

# Answers

## Pages 62–63

**Quick Test**

1. Understanding of the whole text, specific analysis and terminology, awareness of the relevance of context, a well-structured essay and accurate writing.
2. Planning focuses your thoughts and allows you to produce a well-structured essay.
3. Quotations give you more opportunities to do specific AO2 analysis.

**Exam Practice**

Ideas might include the following: he is admired by other animals; he is hard-working and strong; he is brave in the battles; he is loyal and committed; he bears suffering nobly; he is finally defiant. On the other hand: he does not question; he accepts the leadership of the pigs; he is complicit in Napoleon's rise to power; his solution to everything is to work harder rather than confront problems; he does not give leadership. He might be seen as a tragic hero because his flaws have led to his death but these flaws have also harmed others.

## Pages 66–67 and 72–73

**Exam Practice**

Use the mark scheme below to self-assess your strengths and weaknesses. Work up from the bottom, putting a tick by things you have fully accomplished, a ½ by skills that are

in place but need securing and underlining areas that need particular development. The estimated grade boundaries are included so you can assess your progress towards your target grade.

## Pages 68–69

**Quick Test**

1. Understanding of the whole text, specific analysis and terminology, awareness of the relevance of context, a well-structured essay and accurate writing.
2. Planning focuses your thoughts and allows you to produce a well-structured essay.
3. Quotations give you more opportunities to do specific AO2 analysis.

**Exam Practice**

Ideas might include the following: revolution is the only way to achieve freedom and equality; Old Major inspires the animals to revolt; revolution involves taking ownership; the pigs develop Animalism as a revolutionary way of living; after revolution, the animals have to deal with practical problems; the pigs betray the revolution; reasons for the revolution failing; the pigs' corruption; the other animals' stupidity and gullibility; parallels with Russian Revolution; other revolutions from French Revolution to the 'Arab Spring' follow similar patterns; must revolution always fail?

| Grade | AO1 (12 marks) | AO2 (12 marks) | AO3 (6 marks) | AO4 (4 marks) |
|---|---|---|---|---|
| 6–7+ | A convincing, well-structured essay that answers the question fully. Quotations and references are well-chosen and integrated into sentences. The response covers the whole novel. | Analysis of the full range of Orwell's methods. Thorough exploration of the effects of these methods. Accurate range of subject terminology. | Exploration is linked to specific aspects of the novel's contexts to show a detailed understanding | Consistent high level of accuracy. Vocabulary and sentences are used to make ideas clear and precise. |
| 4–5 | A clear essay that always focusses on the exam question. Quotations and references support ideas effectively. The response refers to different points in the novel. | Explanation of Orwell's different methods. Clear understanding of the effects of these methods. Accurate use of subject terminology. | References to relevant aspects of context show a clear understanding. | Good level of accuracy. Vocabulary and sentences help to keep ideas clear. |
| 2–3 | The essay has some good ideas that are mostly relevant. Some quotations and references are used to support the ideas. | Identification of some different methods used by Orwell to convey meaning. Some subject terminology. | Some awareness of how ideas in the novel link to its context. | Reasonable level of accuracy. Errors do not get in the way of the essay making sense. |